Yosemite, the Big Trees, and the High Sierra

YOSEMITE THE BIG TREES AND THE HIGH SIERRA

A Selective Bibliography

BY FRANCIS P. FARQUHAR

UNIVERSITY OF CALIFORNIA PRESS

Berkeley and Los Angeles · 1948

UNIVERSITY OF CALIFORNIA PRESS
BERKELEY AND LOS ANGELES
CALIFORNIA

CAMBRIDGE UNIVERSITY PRESS
LONDON, ENGLAND

PRINTED IN THE UNITED STATES OF AMERICA
BY THE UNIVERSITY OF CALIFORNIA PRESS

TO

HENRY RAUP WAGNER

ILLUSTRIOUS EXPONENT
OF THE ART OF BIBLIOGRAPHY

Preface

MY ORIGINAL PURPOSE in gathering the information presented in this book was to provide accurate descriptions of the more important printed source materials for a history of Yosemite, the Big Trees, and the High Sierra. But as the work progressed it seemed desirable to supplement the bibliographical descriptions with notes on the origin of the respective books and pamphlets and to expand the work still further by comments on significant portions of their contents. This led to a good many references to publications that for one reason or another did not require the full descriptions accorded to the selected titles. The result is a compendium of information designed to be helpful to those who desire to write about the subjects covered and to serve as a useful reference book for librarians and collectors.

The basis of selection of the twenty-five titles has been in part their rarity and unusual character, and in part their originality and importance as contributions to knowledge of the subjects with which they are concerned. It may be asked, Why has the list been closed at twenty-five titles? The limitation is, of course, an arbitrary one; but in examining other titles for possible inclusion I found very few that seemed to fulfill both requirements—unusual character and important contents. Those who wish to search further into the sources of history in this field will naturally consult as guides such well-known books as *One Hundred Years in Yosemite,* by Russell, *Big Trees,* by Fry and White, and perhaps my own compilation, *Place Names of the High Sierra.* These scarcely need bibliographical description and comment—at least so early in their young lives. The files of the *Sierra Club Bulletin* and *Yosemite Nature Notes* will also, of course, be consulted.

The whole category of technical books and papers on geology, botany, and natural history has been omitted from the present compilation.

These fields have their own lists, and the comments they require are quite different from those pertaining to the titles in the present list. Another exclusion is a geographical one: the region north of Yosemite National Park, including Lake Tahoe and the passes north and south of it. Although there are publications of importance and of bibliographical interest that concern this region, they seem to me to fall into a field of interest definitely outside of that of the present discussion.

In the presentation of the bibliographical descriptions I have not attempted to conform to any standardized style. Nevertheless, I believe that the methods used will serve the purpose of identification. Abbreviations have been generally avoided, since the list is not long enough to require the maximum of economy in that respect. In measuring the copies observed I have used a fair approximation of the height and width of the pages. The maps are measured from the outer printed borders or from the extremities of the printed matter, without regard to margins.

To the librarians and collectors who have generously assisted me by answering questions and by displaying or photographing their copies for me, I wish to express my thanks and appreciation. Most of them have been mentioned in the text.

FRANCIS P. FARQUHAR

Berkeley, California,
September, 1948

Contents

Illustrations

1 *Zenas Leonard's Narrative*

a

Narrative of the adventures of Zenas Leonard, a native of Clearfield County, Pa. Who spent five years in trapping for furs, trading with the Indians, &c., &c., of the Rocky Mountains: Written by himself.

Printed and published by D. W. Moore, Clearfield, Pa. 1839.

Pp. iv + 87. 23 × 15½ cm. Boards.

b

Leonard's Narrative. Adventures of Zenas Leonard. Fur trader and trapper. 1831–1836. Reprinted from the rare original of 1839. Edited by W. F. Wagner, M.D. With maps and illustrations.

Cleveland. The Burrows Brothers Company. 1904.

Pp. 317; 2 plates (portraits of Cerré and Walker); 2 illustrations in text (including facsimile of title page of original edition); 1 map in text (Franciscan Missions of California); 1 folding map (Route of Zenas Leonard, 1831–1835; 21 × 31 cm.). 22 × 15½ cm. Blue cloth.

c

[Title same as *a,* except "Penna." for "Pa."]

[Cover Title.] A narrative of the adventures of Zenas Leonard. [Printer's design.] Compliments of the Raftsman's Journal. [Clearfield, Pa.] 1908.

Pp. 106 (t.p. is p. 1.). 21 × 15 cm. Blue paper wrappers, printed on front only.

d

The Lakeside Classics. Narrative of the adventures of Zenas Leonard. Written by himself. Edited by Milo Milton Quaife, secretary and editor of the Burton Historical Collection.

Chicago. The Lakeside Press. R. R. Donnelley & Sons Co. Christmas, 1934.

Pp. xiv + 278; folding map ("Leonard Country"; 17 × 25 cm.). 17 × 11 cm. Red cloth.

Leonard's narrative is the principal source of information about the expedition of Joseph Reddeford Walker, in 1833, from Great Salt Lake to California. Walker's was the first party to use the Humboldt River route to California and the first known party of white men to cross the Sierra Nevada from east to west. Although Leonard's narrative is in the form of a journal, parts of it were obviously rewritten or interpolated at the time of publication. It cannot, therefore, be taken as a precise day-by-day description of the topographical features. Yet, in spite of its gaps and vaguenesses here and there, the reader can follow the route most of the way. Some of the descriptions are unmistakable, and there can be little doubt that Leonard was one of those of Walker's party who were the first white men to look upon Yosemite Valley and to be confronted with that amazing arboreal phenomenon, the Big Tree of the Sierra Nevada.

These episodes are discussed in "Walker's Discovery of Yosemite," by Francis P. Farquhar, in the *Sierra Club Bulletin*, 1942, Vol. 27, No. 4, pp. 35–49, in which are listed the principal sources of information other than Leonard's narrative, of which the following are the most important: "The Rocky Mountains: or, Scenes, Incidents, and Adventures in the Far West; digested from the journal of Captain B. L. E. Bonneville, of the Army of the United States, and illustrated from various other sources," by Washington Irving, 2 vols., Philadelphia, 1837; author's revised edition of the same, entitled "The Adventures of Captain Bonneville, U. S. A., in the Rocky Mountains and the Far West. Digested from his journal and illustrated from various other sources," New York, 1850; "The Life and Adventures of George Nidever (1802–1883)," edited by William Henry Ellison, Berkeley, 1937; Memoir of Joseph R. Walker, in *The Pioneer*, San Jose, September 1, 1877; Memoir of Joseph R. Walker, in *The Sonoma Democrat*, Santa Rosa, November 25, 1876; and

"West Wind, The Life Story of Joseph Reddeford Walker, Knight of the Golden Horseshoe," by Douglas S. Watson, Los Angeles, 1934.

Zenas Leonard was born in Clearfield County, Pennsylvania, in 1809. His career in the fur trade began in 1831, when he enlisted in the Grant and Blackwell party. In 1836 he settled in Jackson County, Missouri, where he died, at Sibley, in 1857. (See, in the *Dictionary of American Biography,* article by W. J. Ghent.)

After five years in the West with the exploring and fur-trading companies of Bonneville, Walker, and others, Leonard returned to his native Clearfield County, Pennsylvania, where four years later, in 1839, his narrative appeared in book form. The publisher, in a preface, says: ". . . it was never published entire, until we procured the manuscript last winter and gave it to the public through the columns of a public newspaper during the past season. The great interest the public took in it, was satisfactorily illustrated by the increase and demand for the paper in which it was published. A number of persons sent in their names as subscribers from all the adjoining counties, besides others more distant—many of whom we were unable to accommodate. From this evidence, as well as the repeated solicitations from every quarter, we have been induced to re-print it, and now offer it to the public in a more convenient form." A footnote by Dr. W. F. Wagner, in *b* identifies the local newspaper as the *Clearfield Republican.* However, that was not the name of the paper at that time, according to an unpublished bibliography and location list in the files of the Historical Society of Western Pennsylvania. (Letter of May 23, 1946.) From 1836 to 1839 it was the Clearfield *Banner,* and from 1839 to 1849 the Clearfield *Democratic Banner.* From the location list it appears that no continuous runs of this period are known to exist. I have found no reference to any copy of an issue that contains any portion of Leonard's narrative. The 1839 edition, *a,* is set in columns two to a page, an indication that the original newspaper type was used.

Copies of *a* are rare. I have examined those in the California Historical Society, the Huntington Library, the Library of the University of California at Los Angeles, and the collections of Dr. George D. Lyman, San

Francisco, and of T. W. Streeter, Morristown, New Jersey. There are copies in the Library of Congress, the Clements Library at the University of Michigan, and the Newberry Library, Chicago. It is listed in Wagner-Camp, No. 75; and in *The Zamorano Eighty*, No. 50, with notes by Henry R. Wagner.

The 1904 edition, *b*, contains an introduction and extensive notes by Dr. W. F. Wagner, dated Washington, D.C. Dr. Wagner later lived in Hartleton, Union County, Pennsylvania. (Not related to Dr. Henry Raup Wagner, of San Marino.) There were 520 copies printed.

There is a copy of *c* in Huntington Library. It is a verbatim reprint of *a*, on a poor grade of paper. The only differences noted are the addition of "D. W. Moore, 1839" after "The Publisher" at end of Preface, and the following: "Reproduced by M. L. McQuown, 1908, by courtesy of A. L. Forcey." I am informed by Mr. Everett D. Graff, of Chicago, that the *Raftsman's Journal* is a weekly newspaper that has been published in Clearfield, Pennsylvania, since 1854.

The Lakeside Press edition, *d*, one of R. R. Donnelley & Sons Co.'s Christmas gift books, is handiest for reading.

A new edition, with notes that will incorporate the results of recent investigations, is much to be desired.

2 *The Great California Tree*

Description of the great tree, recently felled upon the Sierra Nevada, California, now placed for public exhibition, in the spacious Racket Court of the Union Club, No. 596 Broadway, adjoining the Metropolitan Hotel, New York.

New York: Herald Job Printing Office. 1854.

Pp. 8., including cover. 24 × 15½ cm.

Contents. P. 1 (cover)—The Great California Tree. Over 3000 years old—ninety feet in circumference. [Cut of lower portion of huge tree, with figures of persons and lesser trees.] Now exhibiting at No. 596 Broadway, near Niblo's. Admission . . . 25 cents, children . . . half-price. Hours of exhibition from 9 A.M., till 10 P.M. P. 2—Blank. P. 3—Title page. Pp. 4–5—The Great Tree of the Sierra Nevada, California. [Description.] Pp. 6–8—Excerpts from the *Illustrated London News* of February 11 and *Gleason's Pictorial* of October 10.

Although Zenas Leonard (*Title 1*) was the first to describe in print the Big Tree of the Sierra, and although many others doubtless saw these trees in one or more of the groves from the Calaveras to the Kings in the years that followed, the discovery to the world did not occur until 1852, when a hunter named Dowd persuaded some of the miners from Murphy's Camp to follow him and see the sight for themselves. The trees became famous and people flocked to see them. J. M. Lapham pre-empted the land and built a cabin. James L. Sperry then bought out Lapham and built a hotel. There are many accounts of the cutting down of the biggest of the trees, the use of its stump for a dance floor and part of its trunk for a bowling alley, and the stripping off of bark for exhibition purposes (Hutchings, in *Titles 4* and *18;* Whitney, in *Title 7;* and in *Titles* 3 and 9, as well as in this title), yet the story remains confused and contradictory. An unpublished manuscript written years later by

DESCRIPTION

OF THE

GREAT TREE,

RECENTLY FELLED UPON THE SIERRA NEVADA,

CALIFORNIA,

NOW PLACED FOR

PUBLIC EXHIBITION,

In the spacious Racket Court of the Union Club,

NO. 596 BROADWAY,

ADJOINING THE METROPOLITAN HOTEL,

NEW-YORK.

NEW YORK:
HERALD JOB PRINTING OFFICE
1854.

Title page, *Description of the Great Tree*

a member of Dowd's party, however, helps to set the record straight. John de Laittre, of Minneapolis, writing in 1910, says:

"Before Lapham sold out, Captain [W. H.] Hanford... conceived the idea of felling the big tree.... Before felling the tree Mr. Hanford took off the bark in sections; I think sixty feet in height was taken off in ten-foot sections—each section being numbered so that it would fit together as it was originally on the tree. This was all boxed and hauled to Stockton; then sent by steamer to San Francisco, and shipped to New York around Cape Horn. This was an enterprise Captain Hanford conceived himself with the aid of two gentlemen who had made their money in mining in Murphy's Camp by the name of Kimball and Cutting... The idea was to exhibit the tree in New York City, with the expectation, of course, of making money out of it. Captain Hanford went East about the time the bark was to arrive in New York and tried [unsuccessfully] to make arrangements with P. T. Barnum.... He rented a building on Broadway..., took out two floors of the building and set up the tree. He also had a section of the wood, in addition to the bark.... It proved a disastrous venture for the Captain and his friends. Finally, the bark was stored in a warehouse, preparatory to shipping to Paris, and was later destroyed by fire."

Returning to the title under discussion, we find in it the following: "Of this vegetable monster, fifty feet of the bark from the lower part of the trunk is put in natural form for the exhibition. It was first exhibited in San Francisco, and has never been shown in any other place, except the Racket Court, adjoining the Metropolitan Hotel, Broadway, New York. The tree at the Crystal Palace is two thirds smaller in diameter than this, and is not even half as large as the old sycamore, exhibited in this city some twenty years ago." Whence came this diminutive rival? Was it a California Big Tree? Perhaps it was a fake concocted by Barnum. We shall presently see (*Title* 3) that the bark from another tree was set up in the New York Crystal Palace, but this bark was not taken from the tree until 1854, and did not reach New York until July, 1855. At all events, the exhibit at the Racket Court seems to be the one described by de Laittre, for the following statement tallies closely with his: "Previous to felling this immense tree, the bark was stripped from it for the length of fifty feet from the base . . . It was taken off in sections, so that it can be placed relatively in its original position, and thus give the beholder a just idea of the gigantic dimensions of the tree. . . . A piece of wood will be shown which was cut from the tree across the whole diameter. . . . This is the identical tree described in the February [1854] number of the *London Illustrated News, Gleason's Pictorial* for October last [1853], and noticed by the leading scientific journals . . ."

This little folder of eight pages appears to be the first publication, exclusive of newspapers and periodicals, devoted to the Big Tree of California. It is noteworthy in other respects, as well; for besides giving a tolerably good description of the gigantic aspects of the tree, amply borne out by the cut, it introduces a novel botanical name. The publisher, who is presumably the proprietor, takes the liberty of calling his specimen "*Americus Gigantea.*" He does not stop there, however, for to give currency to his name he commits forgery in quoting from the *Illustrated London News* of February 11, 1854. That honest sheet contains extracts from *The Gardners' Chronicle* of December 24, 1853, in which the horticultural editor, Professor Lindley, proposes the name "*Wellingtonia Gigantea*" and follows with a botanical description. In transcribing these extracts, our New York exhibitor substitutes, without a hint of his effrontery, his own "*Americus Gigantea*" and continues to substitute "*Americus*" wherever "*Wellingtonia*" appears in the *Chronicle.* He refrains, and I think quite properly for an American, from including Professor Lindley's highly insular remark: "Wellington stands as high above his contemporaries as the Californian tree above all the surrounding foresters."

The controversy over the scientific name of the Big Tree still burns, although with diminishing heat. *Wellingtonia gigantea* and its inevitable Americanism *Washingtonia gigantea* went out the window when the Frenchman Decaisne identified the tree as a *Sequoia.* His *Sequoia gigantea,* however, was challenged by the phytologists and Lindley was accorded by them half solace in the name *Sequoia Wellingtonia,* which, with the weight of Sargent's *Silva of North America* behind it, still holds legal for many botanists. To be sure, it was gallantly challenged by Sudworth, of the U. S. Forest Service, whose *Sequoia Washingtoniana* was for a long time official for U. S. governmental agencies. But with the passing of Sudworth his authority departed, and *Sequoia gigantea* is now in official use. The latter has also come to prevail among American botanists—Abrams, Eastwood, Jepson, McMinn, among others. A little flurry over the name *Sequoiadendron giganteum* does not seem to have disturbed them. ("The names of the Giant Sequoia: a discussion," by William A. Dayton, in *Leaflets of Western Botany,* San Francisco, April 30, 1943, Vol. 3, No. 10.) Our showman-publisher's *"Americus Gigantea,"* alas, never reached first base.

Although much has been written about the derivation of the name *sequoia* from *Sequoya, Sikwayi,* or *Sequoyah,* the Indian name of the Cherokee half-breed George Gist (Guest, or Guess), who invented an alphabet and mode of writing for the Cherokee language, no evidence has been produced to prove that Endlicher, when in 1847 he gave the name *Sequoia sempervirens* to the coast redwood, had the Indian name in mind. The conjecture has, nevertheless, been almost universally accepted.

Sabin lists this pamphlet in Vol. V, No. G 19720, which indicates that it was in the library of A. W. Griswold. I am unable to find out what became of the Griswold copy. None of the libraries consulted has a copy. The description is taken from my own copy. Sabin, Vol. III, No. 10012, also gives a title taken from the cover of this pamphlet and describes it as having 83 pages. This is obviously a misprint for "8 pages." The two numbers refer to the same publication.

DESCRIPTION OF THE
MAMMOTH TREE FROM CALIFORNIA,
NOW ERECTED AT THE
CRYSTAL PALACE, SYDENHAM

1—Whole Height of Tree . 363 Feet
2.—Height to First Limb . . . 140 Feet
3—Diameter at Base . . . . 31 Feet
4.—Diameter 100 Feet from the Base . 15 Feet
5.—Bark at Base . 18 Inches in Thickness
6.—Bark Removed to the Height of 116 Feet.

Cover, *Description of the Mammoth Tree* (London)

3 *Mammoth Tree at Crystal Palace*

Description of the mammoth tree from California, now erected at the Crystal Palace, Sydenham.

London: Printed by R. S. Francis, Catherine Street, Strand. [N.d., but internal evidence indicates 1857.]

Pp. 24. 21½ × 13½ cm. Pale pink paper wrappers.
Title is on front cover, which also contains engraving of tree surrounded by scaffold with men cutting, and table of dimensions.

Contents. P. 1–Cut of full tree, with scaffold. At top, description of the "Mother of the Forest"; at bottom: "The Engraving on the cover represents a section of the butt of the tree, with the scaffolding around it, after the Bark had been removed. . . . It was engraved from a Daguerreotype taken on the spot, and is a faithful and accurate representation of this Monarch of the Woods." P. 2–Printer's imprint. Pp. 3–9–Description of the mammoth tree from California. [Text, with three cuts.] Pp. 10–19–Extracts from the London press (1856, 1857). Pp. 21–24–Extracts from the New York press (1855).

To provide material for the exhibit described in this pamphlet a second tree in the Calaveras Grove, known as "The Mother of the Forest," was destroyed. In the summer of 1854 the bark was removed to a height of 116 feet. There are a number of illustrations of this stripped tree. The earliest I have noted is a printed letter sheet, 27 × 21 cm., published by James M. Hutchings in 1854. From the same woodcut another sheet, "Die Mammoth-Bäume," text in German, was published by Hutchings & Rosenfield, not dated. A similar sheet, but with a different cut, was published by D. A. Plecker in 1855. In 1855 Thomas A. Ayres made sketches in the Grove which were drawn on stone by Kuchel & Dresel and were printed by Britton & Rey, 1855, on a sheet approximately 45 × 65 cm. (See *California on Stone,* by Harry T. Peters, New York, 1935, p. 143 and plate 74.) In these representations the tree appears vigorous at the top, but in 1861, when Edward Vischer saw it, it was "a mere skeleton." (*Title 5.*) For years it stood thus until fire and storm brought it to earth. In the subject pamphlet the height of the tree is given as 363 feet, but Hutchings, on the letter sheet, gives it as 310 and later, in *Title 4,* as 321. The Whitney Survey found it to be 315 feet. Even at 310 feet it was one of the tallest of known specimens.

The exhibit, like the one described in *Title 2,* was shipped round the Horn to New York. The following remarks are selected from "Extracts from the New York Press," quoted in the pamphlet: "The monarch of the California forest, supposed to be the largest tree in the world, has arrived at this port, from San Francisco, and will be exhibited in the Crystal Palace–the only building in New York large enough to contain it–on and after the 4th of July [1855]."–*New York Tribune.* "The *Washingtonea Gigantea* (so named by botanists) is of much larger dimensions than the specimen of the same genus described and depicted in the *Illustrated London News,* under the title of the *Wellingtonea Gigantea.* . . . The 'big tree' exhibited in this city, several months ago, was almost a pigmy in comparison with this mastodon."–*New York Daily Express.* There are other eloquent notices too extensive for inclusion here, but the following certificate of Mr. Adams can hardly be omitted: "This is to certify that I, Alvin Adams, of the firm of Adams & Co.'s Express, resident of the city of Boston, did on or about the 20th day of June, 1854, visit the grove of mammoth trees in Calaveros County, California. I also certify that I at that time saw trees of immense size, one of which was over 30 feet in diameter. At the time I visited the said grove, Mr. Trask was engaged in taking the bark from one for the purpose of exhibiting it in the Atlantic States and Europe, and to the best of my knowledge and belief, the one now on exhibition at the Crystal Palace in the city of New York, is the same identical tree which I then saw, the bark of which I know to have been removed. Given under my hand and seal this 15th day of August, 1855. Alvin Adams."

Although Hutchings says that the bark was stripped by Mr. George Gale, it appears that the proprietor of the exhibit was Mr. George L.

Trask, who is not to be confused with Dr. John B. Trask, geologist, surveyor, and mapmaker. In the spring of 1856, Trask brought some of his tree bark to London. The "Extracts from the London Press" establish the fact that a portion of the tree about 16 feet high was on private view at the Philharmonic Rooms, Newman Street, Oxford Street. By June it had been moved to the Adelaide Gallery, Strand. "Unfortunately, in London no building could be found high enough to permit of the monster being exhibited to the full height of 116 feet. . . . Could not arrangements be made to have this vegetable wonder reared under the great transept of the Crystal Palace at Sydenham, where the public could see it to advantage?"—*Morning Advertiser*. The answer was, Yes. *The Times* of April 10, 1857, mentions the great crowd that came "to gaze upon that colossal specimen of Transatlantic vegetation" at the tropical end of the building. It remained there until December, 1866, when the Crystal Palace was destroyed by fire.

An interesting account of the propagation of the tree in Great Britain from seeds imported by Veitch and other horticultural suppliers is to be found in *The Pinetum Britannicum: A Descriptive Account of Hardy Coniferous Trees Cultivated in Great Britain*, Edinburgh and London, 1884, 3 vols., known also as "Lawson's Pinetum Britannicum."

There is a copy of the pamphlet in the Huntington Library, and one in my own collection.

4 *Hutchings' Scenes of Wonder and Curiosity*

a

Scenes of wonder and curiosity in California. Illustrated by ninety-two well executed engravings, including the mammoth trees of Calaveras; caves and natural bridges; the Yo-Semite valley; the mammoth trees of Mariposa and Frezno; Mount Shasta; the quicksilver mines of New Almaden and Henriquita; the Farallone islands; the Geyser springs, etc. By J. M. Hutchings. [Two lines quoted from Bayard Taylor.]

San Francisco. Hutchings & Rosenfield, publishers, Montgomery Street. [N.d.]

On verso of title page: "Entered according to Act of Congress, in the year one thousand eight hundred and sixty, by Hutchings & Rosenfield, in the Clerk's office of the District Court of the United States, for the Northern District of California."

Pp. 236 (t.p. is p. 1). 23 × 14½ cm. Black (slate, or blue-green) cloth; title on spine, SCENES/ IN/ CALIFORNIA/ HUTCHINGS, in gold; ornamentation blind-stamped on front and back.

There are actually 93 illustrations; the one on p. 33 is not listed.

b

Scenes of wonder and curiosity in California. Illustrated by ninety-two well finished engravings, executed principally by Thomas Armstrong from drawings by Nahl Brothers, H. Eastman, and P. Loomis; including the mammoth trees of Calaveras; the natural caves and bridges of Calaveras and El Dorado; the Yo-Semite valley; the mammoth trees of Mariposa and Frezno; Mount Shasta the quicksilver mines of New

Almaden and Henriquita; the Farallone islands; the Geyser springs, etc. A study of the Wonderful in Nature lifts us nearer to the Infinite.

San Francisco. Hutchings & Rosenfield, publishers, Montgomery Street. 1861.

Pp. 236 (t.p. is p. 1). 23 × 14½ cm. Blue (or red) cloth, or maroon (or blue) leather: title on spine same as *a;* elaborate gold-stamped ornamentation, front, back and spine; all edges gilt. Also: dark green, blind-stamped, no gilt except title on spine, same as *a*. Text, in all respects save title page, same as *a*.

c

Scenes of wonder and curiosity in California. Illustrated by 105 well executed engravings, including the mammoth trees of Calaveras; the caves and natural bridges of Calaveras; the Yo-Semite valley; the mammoth trees of Mariposa and Frezno; Mount Shasta; the quicksilver mines of New Almaden and Henriquita; the Farallone islands, the Geyser springs, the Riffle-box waterfall, Deer Creek; Lake Bigler; scenes on the Sacramento; the El Dorado County cave, etc.

Published by J. M. Hutchings & Co., San Francisco. 1861.

Pp. 267 (t.p. is p. 1). 23 × 15 cm. Brown leather; title on spine, SCENES/ OF/ WONDER/ AND/ CURIOSITY/ IN/ CALIFORNIA/ HUTCHINGS, elaborately ornamented in gold; gold ornamentation same as *b* on front and back; all edges gilt. Also: brown cloth, gold on spine; other ornamentation blind-stamped; no gilt edges.

There are three new chapters with corresponding illustrations (nos. 94 to 105). The illustration on p. 10 of *a* and *b* has been transferred to p. 9. Several of the titles in the list of illustrations have been changed. The entry on verso of t.p. reads "... sixty-one, by J. M. Hutchings ..." In other respects the text is the same as *a* and *b*.

d

[Title same as *c*.]

Published by J. M. Hutchings & Co., San Francisco. 1862.

Pp. 267 (t.p. is p. 1). 23 × 15 cm. Blue (or black) cloth; title and decorations, in gold, same as *c;* all edges gilt. (A copy has also been noted on heavier paper, smaller size, 21 × 14½ cm., with slightly different ornamentation.) The text is the same as *c*.

e

Scenes of wonder and curiosity in California. Illustrated by upwards of 100 engravings. By James M. Hutchings.

London: Chapman and Hall, 193, Piccadilly. 1865.

Pp. 267 (t.p. is p. 1). 21½ × 14 cm. Maroon cloth; gold on spine, none on front and back.

Same text and illustrations as *c*, except that the illustration on p. 184 has been redrawn, apparently as a concession to British good taste.

f

Scenes of wonder and curiosity in California. Illustrated with over one hundred engravings. A tourist's guide to the Yo-Semite Valley, the Big Tree groves—the natural caves and bridges—the quicksilver mines of New Almaden and Henriquita—Mount Shasta—the Farralone islands, with their sea lions and birds—the Geyser springs—Lake Tahoe, and other places of interest. Also giving outline map of routes to Yo-Semite and Big Tree groves—tables of distances—rates of fare—hotel charges, and other desirable information for the traveller. By J. M. Hutchings, (of Yo-Semite.)

New York and San Francisco: A. Roman and Company, Publishers. 1870.

Pp. 292 (t.p. is p. 1); frontispiece; errata note on p. 292; 4 pp. of adv. of A. Roman & Co. 21 × 15½ cm. Green cloth; gold lettering on front and spine. The text of several of the chapters has been revised and enlarged, particularly in respect to routes and modes of travel. Chapter xii, formerly "Lake Bigler," is now "Lake Tahoe."

g

[Title same as *f*.]

[Same imprint as *f*, dated 1871.]

Same text as *f*, except that two of the three errata have been corrected and errata note is deleted from p. 292. Brick-red cloth.

Also: copies dated 1872 and 1875; same, 1876, but with addition of a page of "Notes to edition of 1876" following p. 292.

James Mason Hutchings, born in Towcester, England, in 1818, came to America at the age of fifteen. He followed the gold rush to California in 1849 and for several years lived in the mining regions. In 1853 he engaged in his first publishing venture, "The Miner's Ten Commandments," a letter sheet with eleven woodcuts surrounding the text. The earliest issue has the imprint "Orders Addressed Box H, Placerville, El Dorado Co."; but later, beginning in 1854, it was issued from San Francisco. It proved to be very popular and many thousands of copies were sold. With this encouragement Hutchings published other letter sheets comprising mining and Indian scenes, as well as "The Mammoth Trees" referred to in the discussion of *Title 3*. By the end of 1854 he had conceived the idea of a monthly illustrated magazine devoted to California life and scenes. The recently discovered Yosemite Valley was naturally a subject for prime consideration; so, in June, 1855, he engaged the artist Thomas A. Ayres and, with two other companions, set out to examine and record its scenic wonders. From one of Ayres' drawings there was produced in October, 1855, the first view of Yosemite to reach the public—a lithograph drawn on stone by Kuchel & Dresel, printed by Britton & Rey, and published by James M. Hutchings.

An explanation is here in order of the varying forms used by Hutchings and his contemporaries in writing the name of the valley. Bunnell (*Title 15, a,* pp. 61–73; *d,* pp. 69–71) says that in naming it he first used the form "Yo-sem-i-ty" or "Yosemity," but that Lieutenant Moore, in 1852, substituted "e" for the final "y." In the *Daily Alta California,* June 12, 1851, it appears as "Yo-Semety," and in the same paper a year later, June 18, 1852, as "Yeosemoty." In the *San Francisco Herald,* December 2, 1853, it takes the present form, "Yosemite," and doubtless there would have been no further confusion if Hutchings had not reopened the subject. Following his visit in 1855 he adopted the form "Yo-Hamite" for the title of his published lithograph, and in his magazine the following year he used "Yo-Ham-i-te." Ayres, in a letter to the *Alta,* August 6, 1856, uses "Yohemity" although in the caption above it appears as "Yohamite." In his magazine for May, 1859 (Vol. 3, No. 11), Hutchings published a communication from Bunnell, "How the Yo-Semite Valley was Discovered and Named," as a result of which Hutchings accepted "Yo-Semite." He used this form consistently thereafter for many years until he finally dropped the hyphen and made it "Yo Semite." The ultimate concession to "Yosemite" was too much for his stubborn nature. Incidentally, he was able to point out (*Title 18*, p. 61) that the Act of Congress of June 30, 1864, by which the valley was ceded to the State of California, uses his spelling. The cause of the argument lies, of course, in the simple fact that the Indians not only didn't spell, but didn't articulate in a manner that could be reproduced in our orthography. (See references to Merriam and to Powers in Farquhar, *Place Names of the High Sierra*, 1926, p. 109.) Despite the popularity of Hutchings' books, his spelling was not widely adopted, and the present form prevailed, largely owing to the prominence it acquired in the publications of the Whitney Survey (*Titles 6* and *7*).

In July, 1856, the first number of *Hutchings' California Magazine* was issued, published by the firm of Hutchings and Rosenfield, Montgomery Street, San Francisco. It continued monthly for five years, ending with Vol. 5, No. 12, June, 1861. Each volume has an even 576 pages. The paper covers and the pages of advertisements reflect the florid taste of the times in their mixture of type faces. On the title page printed for each volume the title is *Hutchings' Illustrated California Magazine*, but in the separate numbers the word "Illustrated" is not used. A complete bound set is in the Bancroft Library. Opinions differ about the quality of the contents. Hubert Howe Bancroft (*Essays and Miscellany*, pp. 599–600) says, in comparing it with Ewer's *Pioneer:* "James M. Hutchings fancied that he understood the public taste better, and in his *California Magazine*, begun in July 1856, he introduced a larger portion of light matter, with special attention to humorous sketches. The size was somewhat reduced, and the editor's department cut down, but the pages received instead the addition of woodcuts, of a mediocre and at times decidedly trashy stamp, like much of the text." In defense of Hutchings it may be said, however, that in the pages of his magazine there is preserved a good deal of material depicting the life and scenes of California in the decade following the Gold Rush—material notably lacking in Bancroft's works,—especially with respect to Yosemite, the Big Trees, and other scenic wonders, all of which were almost entirely ignored by Bancroft.

By the summer of 1861 Hutchings and his associate, Anthony Rosenfield, seem to have separated. The magazine came into the hands of Joseph E. Lawrence and James Brooks, who were also the proprietors of the *Golden Era.* It continued for a time, with the same cover design, but under the name of *The California Magazine and Mountaineer*—a combination, apparently, with *The California Mountaineer,* which H. S. Brooks had started in January, 1861, in Chinese Camp, Tuolumne County.

Quite ignorant of the opinion that Bancroft would subsequently hold of his cuts and his text, Hutchings, in 1860, gathered together extracts from his magazine and published them in book form. The illustrations in *Scenes of Wonder and Curiosity in California,* edition *a,* are entirely from the cuts used in the first four volumes of the magazine. In the second of the two editions of 1861, *f,* several other illustrations were added from Volume 5.

That *a* is the first edition of the work, I think there is no doubt, although there is no date on the title page. Unaccountably, there is no reference to this publication in the magazine, either in the text or in the advertising pages; nor have I found anything by which to establish the month of publication, except that nothing from Volume 5, which begins in July, 1860, appears in the book. But the character of the binding and the events of the succeeding year seem to me to establish clearly that the edition listed here as *a* preceded the one listed as *b*. In 1861 there were two issues of the book—one, *b,* with the imprint "Hutchings and Rosenfield, Publishers"; the other, *c,* with "Published by J. M. Hutchings & Co." The parting of the ways had come, and Hutchings had evidently carried with him all the cuts from the magazine enterprise and the right to use them. There are two curious differences between the title page of *a* and that of *b*. In *a* the author's name is boldly printed—"J. M. Hutchings"—but in *b* as well as in *c* and *d* it is omitted. Did partner Rosenfield object after the book appeared and insist on anonymity? But why the change from "well executed engravings," in *a*, to "well finished," in *b*, and back to "well executed," in *c*? It looks as if Hutchings, in his own edition in 1861, *c*, now that he was free from Rosenfield, had reasserted his own taste. It was not necessary to restore his name as author, for he was now sole publisher.

Hutchings' subsequent career is discussed under *Title 18*.

5 *Vischer's Mammoth Tree Grove and Pictorial*

a

Vischer's views of California. The Mammoth Tree Grove, Calaveras County, California. And its avenues. Consisting of title page & 12 plates with 25 engravings.

Drawn and published by Edward Vischer, San Francisco, Cal. No. 515 Jackson Street, above Montgomery. L. Nagel, print. C. C. Kuchel, Lith. Typographical work by Agnew & Deffebach, San Francisco. Entered according to Act of Congress in the year 1862 by Edward Vischer in the Clerk's Office of the U. S. District Court for the Northern District of Cal.

The title is taken from the first of 13 cards, 27½ × 34½ cm., contained in a cardboard portfolio, covered with black watered silk, in three pieces attached by tapes and a metal clasp. On the flap of the portfolio is stamped in gold "Vischer's Portfolio of the Mammoth Tree Grove." With the exception of the title page, on which the lithograph has been made directly on the printed card, the lithographed views are pasted on cards upon which the text has previously been printed. The cards are accompanied by a folio sheet, folded to make four pages a little larger than the cards: (1) Title and "Introductory Remarks"; (2) and (3), "Description of Plates"; (4) "Appendix. Extract from Hutching's California Magazine, March, 1859." On the inside of the front and back of the portfolio are: (1) lithographed title page, same as the card; (2), printed, an "Index" and "The Visitors Guide." On the cards there are, in all, 25 views of various sizes. Of the 12 plates (exclusive of title page, which has one view) 9 have one view each, 1 has three views, and 2 have six.

b

The forest trees of California. Sequoia gigantea. Calaveras Mammoth Tree Grove. Photographs, from the original drawings of Edward Vischer, with contributions from various sources.

Edward Vischer. 515 Jackson Street, above Montgomery, San Francisco. Agnew & Deffebach, print. 511 Sansome St. Geo. W. Johnson, phot., 649 Clay St.

Title page, as above; verso blank. Single sheet: "Sequoia gigantea . . . Index"; note at foot by E. Vischer on "The Grizzly Giant of the Mariposa Grove"; verso blank. Single sheet: "Sequoia gigantea," notes on the material for publication signed by Edward Vischer, dated April, 1864; verso blank. A title page, "The Mammoth Tree Grove, Calaveras County, Cal., and its avenues. Published by Edward Vischer. San Francisco: Agnew & Deffebach printers, cor. Sansome and Merchant Sts. 1862"; verso, entry in Clerk's Office, 1862. (This is of smaller size than the other pages, measuring 26½ × 18½ cm.) Pages numbered [1] to 13—actually 14, as the verso of 9 is blank and [10] is the recto of 11. Pages 1–7 contain the same text as pages (2) and (3) of *a*. Pages 10–13 contain brief explanations of views not included in the portfolio, *a*. Appendix, numbered [i] to iii; iv, blank; same text as page (4) of *a*.

Yellow paper covers, front same as title page. 26½ × 21 cm.

This pamphlet appears to be made up of sheets of several different pamphlets, or projected pamphlets, designed to accompany various collections of photographic reproductions. Some examples may exist in other forms or may be combined differently, but the few copies I have seen are the same.

c

Vischer's pictorial of California. Landscape, trees and forest scenes. Grand features of California scenery, life, traffic and customs. Photographs from the original drawings. In five series of twelve numbers each, with a supplement, and contributions from reliable sources.

San Francisco, April, 1870. Printed by Joseph Winterburn & Company, No. 417 Clay Street, between Sansome and Battery Streets.

An inserted title page printed in red (same as regular title page, except that the reference to photographs is omitted); 3 pages printed in purple (gold in special copies), consisting of a poem, "California"; regular title page, with copyright and entry notices dated 1863 and 1867 on verso; table of contents, verso blank; pp. [1]–132; 3 pages printed in red (gold in special copies), containing dedication to the Society of California Pioneers. Inserted after p. 8 are a blank sheet and a page with half title, "Sixty numbers of landscape"; in some copies there are two additional sheets, printed one side only, with lists of views contained in the album. Also inserted at end in some copies are 4 pages of opinions of the press.

There are two sizes: one to accompany the album, 29½ × 23 cm.; the other to accompany a set of views on cards, 23 × 18 cm. The size of type matter is the same in each. The binding is usually brown cloth, with gold lettering and ornamentation. I have a copy, large size, bound in green cloth, at the back of which a folder is bound in, entitled: "Synopsis of Vischer's pictorial of California. Miniature illustrations, landscape, trees and forest scenes, and selections from miscellaneous subjects. Author's complimentary edition for gratifying distant friends." The miniatures are grouped on 9 sheets reduced by photography from larger sheets.

Edward Vischer (1809–1878), a native of Bavaria, first came to California in 1842 on a brief visit from Mexico; he came again, about 1847, to settle in San Francisco. Wherever he went he made sketches. In 1862 he began a series of portfolios and albums illustrated by these sketches—first by lithography, later by photography—accompanied by printed descriptions. ("Edward Vischer and his 'Pictorial of California,' a biographical sketch as told by Hubert Vischer to Francis P. Farquhar in November 1930 and January 1931," 100 copies printed at the Grabhorn Press, San Francisco, 1932; and "Edward Vischer's first visit to California," translated and edited by Erwin Gustav Gudde, in the *California Historical Society Quarterly,* September, 1940, Vol. 19, No. 3, pp. 193–216.) The date of Vischer's death, according to his son Hubert's recollection, was 1879, but a newspaper notice discloses it to be December 24, 1878.

There is a good deal of interesting information about the Big Trees in the Vischer publications, including odds and ends not to be found elsewhere. The descriptions, together with the views, are helpful in establishing the history of the individual trees and the structures erected in the neighborhood. Moreover, the information has the merit of being based on personal observation: Vischer visited the Calaveras Grove in 1859 and again in 1861. Several of the plates and views accompanying *a* and *c* show the stump and log of the tree felled for purposes of display, as well as the tree from which the bark was removed. (See remarks under *Titles* 2, 3, and 9.) Of peculiar interest are the views that show camels among the Big Trees and on the passes of the Sierra. (*a,* Pl. IX; and Nos. 6, 18, 19, 23, 43, and 47 of the *Pictorial,* with corresponding descriptions in *c.*) The camels were imported from the Amoor River, Siberia, and were being taken across the Sierra to the Washoe mines at the time of Vischer's visit to the grove in the fall of 1861. ("Camels in the Sketches of Edward Vischer," by Francis P. Farquhar, in the *California Historical Society Quarterly,* December, 1930, Vol. 9, No. 4, pp. 332–335.)

In addition to the portfolio, *a,* Vischer published on one large sheet a group of 16 of the views, including the one showing the camels, with explanatory text beneath, measuring 52½ × 64 cm., exclusive of borders. The views, with lithographed titles, are printed directly on the same sheet with the typographical main title and explanatory text. The lithography is credited to Nagel, Fishbourne & Kuchel. In the printing, the same stone appears to have been used for the separate prints, although some of these are slightly trimmed, with the exception of No. 11, in the lower right corner, which is redrawn on the stone in a smaller size than the corresponding Plate VIII. (See *California on Stone,* by Harry T. Peters, New York, 1935, p. 169, plate 84.)

In a note on page 95 of *c* the author says: "The lithographic publication was suddenly brought to an end by the breaking of the stone on which the principal plates were drawn." Thereafter, Vischer abandoned the lithographic process, which had, in fact, proved unsatisfactory as a means of presenting his work, and turned to photography for the reproduction of his sketches and supplementary matter. He made several albums of views exclusively of the Mammoth Tree Grove, adding to his own sketches those of T. A. Ayres and others, as well as photographs made by Don Rafael Ordoñez Castro, "of the Pacific Squadron of Spain," who visited the Grove in the fall of 1863.

In the text, *c,* to accompany the *Pictorial,* there are, besides references to the Big Trees, a number relating to the region around Lake Tahoe, the American River, and other parts of the Sierra. The *Pictorial* itself was issued in several forms. A prospectus in Dr. George D. Lyman's collection, dated June 20, 1870, states: "The Pictorial is, thus far, represented by only twenty copies, completed to fulfill engagements to original subscribers." Further subscriptions are solicited, with a choice of four forms of publication: 100 plates, bound in half morocco, $50; 120 plates mounted on bristol board, unbound, $50; 120 plates full morocco, superior finish, $75; set of 100 photographs, unmounted, with pamphlet, $40. How many were sold is not known, but the costly nature of the work and the difficulty of procuring uniform sets of prints indicate that the number was small, an indication borne out by the present scarcity of examples of Vischer's work.

Vischer issued several other publications, the most noteworthy of which are: "Sketches of the Washoe Mining Region: Photographs Reduced from Originals, Twenty-five Numbers," San Francisco: Valentine & Co., 1862, a pamphlet of 24 pages accompanying a portfolio of views; and, "Missions of Upper California, 1872. Notes on the California Missions, a Supplement to Vischer's Pictorial of California, Dedicated to Its Patrons," San Francisco: Winterburn & Co., 1872, 44 + viii + iv pages. The latter appears in several sizes and styles of typography; a few albums of views of the missions are known to have been made.

6 *Whitney Survey's Geology*

Geological Survey of California, J. D. Whitney, State Geologist.

Geology. Volume I. Report of Progress and Synopsis of the Field-Work from 1860 to 1864.

Published by authority of the Legislature of California. 1865.

Printed by Caxton Press of Sherman & Co., Philadelphia.

Pp. xxvii + 498; 9 plates, of which the frontispiece is plate 7; 81 figures in text. 26½ × 19 cm. Green cloth, gold ornament on front cover; gold lettering on spine.

The Geological Survey of California was instituted by an act of the Legislature approved April 21, 1860. By Section One of the Act, J. D. Whitney was appointed State Geologist. Work was begun in December, 1860, and was prosecuted vigorously during the next four years, with William H. Brewer in charge of field parties. Thereafter, for lack of appropriations, the work was intermittent until the discontinuance of the Survey in 1873. The results of the Survey were embodied in a series of reports and maps, never completed, and its value was projected into the future through the training of such men as Clarence King, James T. Gardner (who later spelled his name Gardiner), and Charles F. Hoffmann, all of whom made many contributions in later years in the field of geology and topography. The work of the Survey is summarized in *Life and Letters of Josiah Dwight Whitney,* by Edwin Tenney Brewster, Boston and New York, 1909, and in the Introduction to *Up and Down California in 1860–1864: The Journal of William H. Brewer,* edited by Francis P. Farquhar, New Haven, 1930. Its publications are listed in *A Bibliography Relating to the Geology, Palaeontology, and Mineral Resources of California,* by Anthony W. Vogdes, Sacramento, 1896.

Geology, Volume I was the second of the Survey's reports to be issued. It contains the first extensive description of the High Sierra to be published, and establishes the definition, "that portion of this great chain which lies above the metalliferous belt just described, forming the crest of the range, and the water-shed between the streams flowing west to the Pacific Ocean and those which find their way eastward into the Great Basin, or some subordinate one, where they are lost by evaporation."

The volume is well illustrated with woodcuts taken from sketches made for the most part by Whitney and Hoffmann, and from photographs made in Yosemite by Watkins. At one time the work of producing the volume was "set back about a month because all the engravers and plate printers have been engaged on Prest. Lincoln's portraits." (Unpublished letter from J. D. Whitney to W. H. Brewer, May 28, 1865.*) Copies were shipped by Sherman & Co. to Whitney, December 21, 1865. (Whitney to Brewer, Dec. 23, 1865.)

In 1882 Whitney was Professor of Geology at Harvard. Although the days of the California Survey were fading into the past, he endeavored to preserve something of the residue of his work by publishing at his own expense, or in conjunction with the Harvard Museum of Comparative Zoology, a *Report on the Fossil Plants of the Auriferous Gravel Deposits of the Sierra Nevada,* by Leo Lesquereux, 1878; his own works on *The Auriferous Gravels of the Sierra Nevada of California,* 1880, and *The Climatic Changes of Later Geological Times,* 1882. Finally, he published a group of papers on coal, bituminous substances, and quicksilver, written some ten years earlier by members of the Survey, as *Geology, Volume II: The Coast Ranges,* which bears the imprint: "Cambridge, Mass.: John Wilson & Son, University Press. 1882." It is a thin book of 148 pages, with 5 plates, 3 of which are heliotype illustrations from photographs by Watkins, and is otherwise uniform in appearance with Volume I.

* The Whitney-Brewer correspondence was deposited in the Bancroft Library in 1947.

7 *Whitney's Yosemite Book and Guide Books*

a

Geological Survey of California. J. D. Whitney, State Geologist. The Yosemite book; a description of the Yosemite valley and the adjacent region of the Sierra Nevada, and of the big trees of California. Illustrated by maps and photographs.

Published by authority of the Legislature. New York, Julius Bien. 1868.

Pp. 116 (h.t. is p. 1); 28 plates (photographs); 2 maps. 30 × 25 cm. Half leather, maroon (or green) cloth; ornamental gold lettering on front; gold ornamentation on spine; all edges gilt. Heavy paper, wide margins. Photographs on linen hinges.

Map 1. Map of the Yosemite Valley from surveys made by order of the Commissioners to manage the Yosemite Valley and Mariposa Big Tree Grove by C. King and J. T. Gardner. 1865. Drawn by J. T. G. Scale: 1 mile to 2 inches. 39 × 64 cm. (The level portions of the Valley are colored green.)

Map 2. Map of a portion of the Sierra Nevada adjacent to the Yosemite Valley from surveys made by Chs. F. Hoffmann and J. T. Gardner, 1863–1867. Scale: 2 miles to 1 inch. 53 × 77 cm.

b

Geological Survey of California. J. D. Whitney, State Geologist. The Yosemite guide-book: a description of the Yosemite valley and the adjacent region of the Sierra Nevada, and of the big trees of California, illustrated by maps and wood cuts.

Published by authority of the Legislature. 1869.

Pp. 155 (h.t. is p. 1); 8 plates, of which the frontispiece is plate 8; 20 figures in text. Supplementary notice, from the *San Francisco Bulletin* of May 28, 1869, inserted facing p. 48. Maps in front and back pockets. 23 × 17 cm. Green cloth, gold ornamentation front, back, and spine.

Maps: same as in *a*, except that there is no coloring.

c

[Same as *b*, except that the date on title page is 1870 and that Map 1 has been redrawn. No "supplementary notice" in any 1870 copy observed.]

d

Geological Survey of California. J. D. Whitney, State Geologist. The Yosemite guide-book: a description of the Yosemite valley and the adjacent region of the Sierra Nevada, and of the big trees of California. With two maps.

Published by authority of the Legislature. 1871.

Pp. 133 (t.p. is p. 1); 2 maps. 16 × 10½ cm. Maroon cloth; gold lettering on face and spine, blind-stamped on back. (Another copy noted lacks lettering on spine; brick-red cloth.)

Map 1. Map of the Yosemite valley prepared to accompany the pocket edition of the Yosemite Guide Book. (State Geologl. Survey.) 1871. Scale 1 mile to 1 inch. 12 × 19½ cm.

Map. 2. Map of the routes from San Francisco to the Yosemite valley prepared to accompany the pocket edition of the Yosemite Guide Book. (State Geol. Survey.) 1871. Scale 12 miles to 1 inch. 12½ × 47 cm.

e

[Same title and text; dated 1871, but maps are new and are dated 1872.] Blue cloth; gold lettering on spine, blind-stamped on face, not on back.

Map 1. Same title as Map 1 in *d;* scale approx. 1 mile to ¾ inch. An entirely new map, dated 1872. 13 × 24 cm.

Map 2. Same title as Map 2 in *d,* but scale 18 miles to 1 inch. An entirely new map, lithographed in color (others are black and white), dated 1872. 14½ × 42 cm.

f

[Same title.] New edition, revised and corrected. With four maps.

Published by authority of the Legislature. 1874.

Pp. 186 (t.p. is p. 1); 3 maps bound in, 1 in back pocket. 15 × 10½ cm. Salmon (or green) cloth; black and gold lettering and ornamentation on front, gold on spine; all edges gilt.

Map 1. Same as Map 2 in *e*, dated 1872.

Map 2. Same title as Map 1 in *e*, same scale, but redrawn, dated 1874. 13 × 24 cm.

Map 3. Sketch of the Hetch-Hetchy Valley. (State Geologl. Survey.) 1874. Scale 2 inches to 1½ miles. 8 × 13½ cm.

Map 4. Similar to Map 2 in *a*, but reduced in scale to 3 miles to 1 inch. 35 × 20½ cm.

By Act of Congress approved June 30, 1864, the Yosemite Valley and the Mariposa Grove of Big Trees were granted by the Federal Government to the State of California. Upon accepting this grant, the Legislature authorized the State Geologist to make certain surveys and to explore the adjacent region for the purpose of preparing a full description of the country. J. D. Whitney, the State Geologist, was appointed by the Governor to be one of the Commissioners to manage the grant. A surveying party which included Clarence King and James T. Gardner [Gardiner] spent the summer of 1866 in the field, and, at the same time, Whitney arranged with Carleton E. Watkins for a series of photographs. It was planned to publish two editions of a book: one to be called the "Yosemite Guide Book," the other, "Yosemite Gift Book," the latter to contain photographs. (See *Title 23, Report of the Commissioners* for 1866–67.) Unpublished letters from Whitney to William H. Brewer disclose that King's work was unsatisfactory. "I have not been able to use his notes at all in the Yosemite Book," says Whitney, December 13, 1868. In an earlier letter, August 27, 1867, he says: "King having made a very unsatisfactory report, I have been obliged to send up a party to finish the work they left undone . . . I have sent with Hoffmann the same photographer (Harris) who took those Oregon views. He is to go to the head of the Tuolumne to take views where Watkins failed to go last year." The results are seen in the four photographs by W. Harris (Pls. XXV to XXVIII), which supplement the 24 views by Watkins in "The Yosemite Book," and the completion by Hoffmann of Map 2.

A note on page 13 of *a* explains the limitation on the number of copies of this edition: "As only a small number of prints could be obtained from the photographic artist, the number of copies of the illustrated volume, or the present 'Yosemite Book,' which could be issued was necessarily limited to 250; another edition, without photographs, but with the maps, and intended to serve as a guide-book to the Yosemite Valley and its surroundings, will appear shortly after the issuing of this volume. It will be called 'The Yosemite Guide-Book.' "

On November 26, 1868, Whitney wrote to Brewer: "I have received the first printed sheets of the Yosemite Book. Even the University Press people are obliged to admit that they never saw anything to beat it." The first copies of the completed book were delivered early in 1869.

The Yosemite Guide-Book, *b* and *c,* was printed by the University Press, Cambridge, and is also a very well printed book. The preface is dated May 1, 1869. The woodcut illustrations were selected from those used in *Geology, Volume I.* The maps in *b* are the same as those in *a,* except that there is no coloring on Map 1. In *c,* however, there are many differences in Map 2. The explanation is found in a letter from Whitney to Brewer, October 10, 1869, in which Whitney says: "Hoffmann and I have just been looking at the map of the Yos. Valley and find that all the part done by King, or pretended to be done by him—namely the bottom of the Valley— has all got to come out and be put in correctly for a new edition, as the whole of King's work there was a complete sham." Map 1 in *a* and *b* was lithographed by N. Y. Lithg. & Prtg. Co.; the revised map in *c* was done by J. Bien, who also did Map 2 in all three editions.

The "pocket editions" *d, e,* and *f* are attractive little volumes, especially the last. They contain a good deal of information that is still useful and are full of interesting historical allusions. Some of the matter relating to the southern portion of the High Sierra, to be found in *d* and *e,* is omitted in *f,* but this is compensated for by a revision of the information about the Yosemite region and by improved maps.

8 *Hittell's Yosemite Guide Book*

Yosemite: its wonders and its beauties. With information adapted to the wants of tourists about to visit the valley. By John S. Hittell. Illustrated with twenty photographic views taken by "Helios," and a map of the valley.

San Francisco: H. H. Bancroft & Company, 609 Montgomery St., and 607–617 Merchant St., New York: 113 William Street. 1868.

Pp. i–viii, 9–59 (t.p. is p. i); 20 plates (photographic prints pasted on leaves with printed legends); map (frontispiece, folded); 3 pp. advs. 18½ × 11 cm. Green cloth, "Yosemite" in gold, on face.

Map: Yosemite Valley. Lith. Britton & Rey, San Francisco. 18 × 20½ cm.

This appears to be the first guide book to Yosemite. It contains liberal quotations from Professor Whitney, Starr King, Horace Greeley, and others, with very little original material. It is noteworthy, however, for the illustrations, which are actual photographic prints, greatly reduced. "Helios" was the celebrated photographer who called himself Edward J. (or Eadward) Muybridge, whose experiments with photographing animal locomotion (*The Horse in Motion,* 1878) led to the cinematograph. His real name was Edward James Muggeridge. He was born in England, 1830, and died there, 1904. (*Dictionary of National Biography.*) Muybridge took many fine photographs of Pacific Coast scenery, including Yosemite, the Big Trees, Oregon, and Alaska.

John Shertzer Hittell (1825–1901), brother of Theodore (1830–1917), is best known for his *The Resources of California* (San Francisco, 1863) and *A History of the City of San Francisco and Incidentally of the State of California* (San Francisco, 1878). In the former there are a few pages of description of Yosemite and of the Big Trees, pp. 73–83. He was a contributor to the *Overland Monthly.* (See *Quarterly of the California Society of Pioneers,* March, 1925.)

In 1871, A. L. Bancroft & Company, San Francisco, published "Bancroft's Tourist's Guide. Yosemite. San Francisco and around the Bay, (South.)" There is no indication of its authorship, and I find no evidence that Hittell wrote it. It was superseded in 1882 by "Bancroft's Pacific Coast Guide Book," with John S. Hittell's name on the title page as author. A revised edition, 1885, is entitled "Hittell's Hand-Book of Pacific Coast Travel," as is a further revision dated 1887. Chapter v, "The Sierra Nevada," which includes Yosemite and the Big Trees, pp. 149–188, is substantially the same in all three editions. The later guide books are of no practical value today and lack the interest that attaches to the pioneer effort of 1868.

9 *Williams' Mammoth Trees*

Mammoth trees of California, illustrated by a comparison with other noted trees, ancient and modern. Compiled by J. Otis Williams, of the Boston Public Library. With a hand-book in brief, for a trip to the Calaveras Groves, and Yo-Semite Valley. [Quotation from L. Agassiz.]

Boston: Alfred Mudge & Son, printers, no. 34 School Street. 1871.

Pp. 55. 23 × 14½ cm. Green paper wrappers. Front cover: same as title page, except vignette of dancing party on big tree stump replaces Agassiz quotation, and "Price, 25 cents" is added at bottom. Back cover: Cut of "The Original Big Tree, Calaveras Grove, California." "Solid section of this tree . . . cut off by Jellerson & Ricker, September, 1870, now on exhibition."

At the end of this pamphlet is "A Card," which presents succinctly the occasion for this publication:

"The section of the 'Original Big Tree,' from Calaveras grove, California, now on exhibition, measuring forty-six (46) feet in circumference, was cut by us, September, 1870, from the log now lying where it fell when the tree was 'bored off' in 1853.

"It is the only solid section of the tree ever brought from California, and shows its diameter and circumference at thirty (30) feet from the ground.

"The exhibition in Boston will continue until March 31, 1871, at Big Tree Cottage, a building erected by us on Court Street, expressly for this purpose, no suitable room having been found in the city high studded enough to admit of the 'setting up' of the section. . . .

"Very Respectfully, Jellerson & Ricker."

The pamphlet describes the method by which Messrs. Jellerson & Ricker obtained the "chip," with "a sort of cross between a gigantic

MAMMOTH TREES

OF

CALIFORNIA,

Illustrated by a Comparison with other Noted Trees,
Ancient and Modern.

COMPILED BY J. OTIS WILLIAMS,
OF THE BOSTON PUBLIC LIBRARY.

WITH A HAND-BOOK IN BRIEF,

For a Trip to the Calaveras Groves, and Yo-Semite Valley.

BOSTON:
ALFRED MUDGE & SON, PRINTERS, No. 34 SCHOOL STREET.
1871.

PRICE, 25 CENTS.

Cover, *Mammoth Trees of California* (Boston)

double plane and a two-handled lumber saw." There is a picture of the operation. The section came to the ground in three or four fragments, which greatly simplified the problem of transportation. From the grove the "fragments" traveled to Stockton on the backs of twelve mules. Just how the load was divided is not stated. They were carried to San Francisco by steamer, and, after a local exhibition, the proprietors and their exhibit "took the cars over the Pacific R.R. for Boston."

From "Opinions of the Press" (pp. 45–58 of this pamphlet) are culled the following items:

"Nobody who has any curiosity to see something of the wonders of nature ought to allow the opportunity of seeing a section of one of the big trees of California to pass unimproved.—L. Agassiz."

"Col. Thomas E. Chickering of piano fame ordered three hundred admission cards for the use of his workmen after an inspection of the tree Wednesday."

"The big tree was examined by nearly every member of the legislature last week, and they unanimously agree that it is a curiosity that should be seen by all their constituents."

"The average attendance has not been much less than a thousand a day."

"As this section is soon to go abroad, the present will probably be the only opportunity of seeing this specimen of the Monarch of the Forest."

This section cut in 1870 was not to be the last of such exhibits. In the Huntington Library is a broadside, "California Big Tree (Sequoia gigantea) 2250 Years Old. 276 Ft. High. 80 Ft. around. . . . On Exhibition at 4232 Elm Avenue." It refers to "an interesting printed history," but I have not found a copy. The occasion and date of the exhibit were the Centennial Exhibition, at Philadelphia, 1876.

In a little folder in my collection, "Sequoia Gigantea. California's Big Trees," compiled by Bert Barton, of Badger, California (date uncertain, but probably about 1922), is found the following: "In 1875 a man by the name of Vivian, conceived the idea of making a fortune by sending a section of one of these trees to the Centennial. He selected one about

75 yards from General Grant. A 16-foot cut was divided into eight sections and the outside shell was taken off and shipped. Upon arrival he cemented the sections together and cut a doorway so that people could go inside. Vivian's dream of riches was not realized." The description tallies with the Huntington Library broadside.

It is interesting to note that John Muir was present at the cutting. He writes: "Here we heard the sound of axes, and soon came upon a group of men busily engaged in preparing a section of one of the big trees they had felled for the Centennial Exhibition." (*Picturesque California,* 1888, Vol. 1, p. 84.) Walter Fry, in *Sequoia National Park Nature Guide Service, Historical Series, Bulletin No. 6,* March 17, 1925, says that the "Centennial" tree in General Grant National Park was felled by John Trout and John Carrington under contract with William and Thomas Vivian, who shipped two 16-foot sections to Philadephia. The stump was 28 feet, 4 inches in diameter.

Another version of the "Centennial" tree is found in *Guide to the Grand and Subline Scenery* (*Title 16*), in which it is said that "One Martin Vivian was arrested in 1876, and found guilty of vandalism in cutting down one of these large trees. He was fined $50 by the Court. He ought to have been imprisoned for life! He cut it down to take to the Centennial at Philadelphia." There is a cut showing a crew in the act of felling the tree. Soon many trees were to be slaughtered in the lumbering operations of Converse Basin and Hume, with no fines for "vandalism."

Barton mentions two other shipments of sections East. In 1886 a tree was felled so that a section might be sent to the Natural History Museum. It measured 28 feet inside the bark. In 1893 a section was sent to the World's Fair at Chicago.

10 *Kneeland's Wonders of the Yosemite Valley*

a

The Wonders of the Yosemite Valley, and of California. Prof. Samuel Kneeland, A.M., M.D., Professor of Zoology in the Massachusetts Institute of Technology. With original photographic illustration, by John P. Soule.

Boston: Alexander Moore. 1871.

Pp. i–xii. Includes 2 flyleaves (i–iv), half title (v), t.p. (vii), dedication (ix), preface (xi–xii), 13–71. 10 photos., 3 figs. in text. 26½ × 17½ cm. Mulberry cloth, elaborate gold lettering on face and spine, blind-stamped on back cover, all edges gilt.

b

[Same title.]

Boston: Alexander Moore. Lee & Shepard. New York: Lee, Shepard & Dillingham. 1872.

Pp. i–xii (same); 13–79. 10 photos.; 3 figs. in text, 2 maps. 26 × 17 cm. Same binding as *a;* also in green cloth.

c

[Same title.] Third edition, revised and enlarged.

(Same imprint as *b*.)

Pp. i–xii (same), 13–98; 10 photos., 3 figs. in text, 2 maps. (The additional matter is not correctly described in the "Index" on p. 98.) 26 × 17 cm. Same binding as *b,* except no lettering on spine.

d

[Same title.] Third edition, revised and enlarged.

(Same imprint as *b* and *c*.)

Same paging and text as *c,* except that the "Index" on p. 98 is correct, and there are 20 photos instead of 10. Binding same as *a,* with a touch of color added.

Samuel Kneeland

This is a very attractive book and is made more interesting by the additional matter incorporated in each successive edition. Kneeland took pains to get reliable information and present it with more than ordinary care. The photographic illustrations are excellent and include some unusual views.

The preface to *a* is dated Boston, November, 1871, but in the other editions the date is omitted. In *b,* besides this omission and the changes in imprint noted, there are additional pages, 73–78, which contain 1872 material and 2 maps printed on unnumbered pages inserted in text. The maps contain no original matter.

The third edition, *c,* has further additions: besides an expansion of the 1872 material, with an account of the author's second visit to Yosemite, there are some pages on Yosemite in winter and an essay on "The Yosemite Glaciers" (pp. 89–97). Of the latter, John Muir wrote to Mrs. Carr (October 8, 1872): "Professor Kneeland, Secretary, Boston Institute of Technology, gathered some letters I sent to Runkle and that 'Tribune' letter, and hashed them into a compost called a paper for the Boston Historical Society, and gave me credit for all of the smaller sayings and doings and stole the broadest truth to himself." (*Letters to a Friend, Title* 22, pp. 134–135.) The paper was read at a meeting of the Boston Society of Natural History, February 21, 1872, and was published in the *Proceedings* of the Society (Vol. 15, 1872, pp. 36–47) before its appearance in *c*. Publication in this manner, while not quite fair to John Muir, had the effect of making known his views to a wider circle than had been reached by publications under his own name. Hence its importance in the development of knowledge of the Sierra Nevada.

The fourth variant of this book, *d,* is the most desirable, as it has all the material of the others with 10 additional photographic illustrations. In one copy noted, five other illustrations, while of the same subjects as those in *a, b,* and *c,* are from different negatives; in another copy, these five are not different, but one of the new illustrations differs slightly from that in the other copy.

No doubt other variations exist.

In none of the copies observed are the illustrations placed consistently opposite the pages called for on the plates. John P. Soule may not have been the actual photographer; he was a publisher with offices in Boston, and may have obtained the prints or negatives from local photographers in Yosemite.

An account of Kneeland's visit to Yosemite was included in a series of "Notes of a Health Trip to the Pacific" (Fourth Paper: "Yosemite Valley") published in *Good Health* (Boston, September, 1871, Vol. 3, pp. 158–162).

Dr. Samuel Kneeland (1821–1888) was born in Boston; received from Harvard the degrees of A.B., 1840, A.M. and M.D., 1843; served as surgeon in the Union Army, 1862–1866; was Secretary of the Massachusetts Institute of Technology from its founding, in 1865, to 1878, and Professor of Zoölogy and Physiology, 1869–1878. He made collecting expeditions to Lake Superior, Brazil, Iceland, Hawaii, and the Philippine Islands, and wrote, besides the Yosemite book, *An American in Iceland,* 1876, and *The Philippine Islands,* 1883. He contributed many articles to Appleton's *American Encyclopedia,* and published many medical papers. He was Secretary of the American Academy of Arts and Sciences and of the Boston Society of Natural History. He died in Hamburg, Germany. (*Proceedinags of the American Academy of Arts and Sciences,* for 1889, n.s., Vol. 16; *Proceedings of the Boston Society of Natural History,* for 1890, Vol. 24.)

11 *Therese Yelverton's Zanita*

Zanita: A tale of Yo-semite. By Therese Yelverton, Viscountess Avonmore.

[Publisher's monogram.]

New York: Published by Hurd and Houghton. Cambridge: Riverside Press. 1872.

Pp. iv + 296. 19 × 12½ cm. Orange cloth.

The lady who styled herself Viscountess Avonmore spent the summer of 1870 in Yosemite, where she attached herself to the Hutchings family and made eyes at John Muir. He escaped to the woods, but not before she had noted enough of his conversation and his ways of life to make him over into Kenmuir, the hero of her novel. Florence Hutchings became Zanita (derived from the shrub, *manzanita*), whose demise by falling from Half Dome into Mirror Lake is the climax of the story. Although the romantic style and manifest absurdities of this novel make it tough going for present-day readers, there are passages here and there that indicate an unexpected sophistication, which a little examination of the author's history will explain.

Nine years before her Yosemite visit she had been the central figure in a spectacular trial in the Court of Common Pleas, Dublin, Ireland, to determine whether Maria Theresa Longworth, otherwise Yelverton, was married or not married to Major William Charles Yelverton. The Judgment was: "Yes, she had been married to him twice—once, in Scotland, again, in Ireland." Yelverton, meanwhile, had married another woman. You see, the story becomes complicated, as was the subsequent litigation. The verbatim testimony in the Dublin trial is worth looking into, despite the diamond type; it may be found in "The Yelverton Marriage Case, Thelwall v. Yelverton, comprising an authentic and unabridged account of the most extraordinary trial of modern times, with all its revelation, incidents, and details specially reported. Illustrated with portraits, views of localities, leading events, and important situations. Price one shilling. London: George Vickers, Angel Court Strand" (1861; pp. 191; ppw.).

Charles Warren Stoddard had some acquaintance with the lady and wrote a chapter about her in his book, *In the Footprints of the Padres* (San Francisco: A. M. Robertson, 1902). This chapter, "A Mysterious History," was omitted from the second edition, 1911. See, also "Summer with a Countess," by Mary Viola Lawrence, in the *Overland Monthly*, November, 1871; and pp. 137–142 in *Son of the Wilderness: The Life of John Muir,* by Linnie Marsh Wolfe (New York: Alfred A. Knopf, 1945). Ella Sterling Cummins, in *The Story of the Files,* San Francisco, 1893, remarks, p. 161: "Viewed from the common-sense point of view, I am afraid she was a little queer, and something of a problem to those who tried to befriend her."

This book has been referred to as dated 1871. That is the date of entry shown on verso of title page and is the date shown on the publisher's records. All copies I have seen, however, have 1872 on the title page. It was reviewed in the *Overland Monthly,* January, 1872. The first and only printing consisted of 2,000 copies.

12 *Clarence King's Mountaineering in the Sierra Nevada*

a

Mountaineering in the Sierra Nevada. By Clarence King. "Altiora petimus."

Boston: James R. Osgood and Company, Lake Ticknor & Fields, and Fields, Osgood, & Co. 1872.

Pp. 292. 20 × 13½ cm. Green (or maroon) cloth; t.e.g. Some copies have publisher's monogram on t.p., others do not. There are large-paper copies, 23 × 15 cm., bound in half leather with marbled end papers, t.e.g., presumably made for author's presentation copies.

b

[Same title.]

London: Sampson Low, Marston, Low, & Searle, Crown Buildings, 188 Fleet Street. 1872. All rights reserved.

Pp. 292. 20½ × 14 cm. Brown cloth; front and spine decorated in gold, decoration and ornamental gold lettering on spine. 32 pp. of advs. bound in at end. Printed in Cambridge [Massachusetts] by Welch, Bigelow, & Co., but bound in England.

c

[Same title.]

London: Sampson Low, Marston, Low, & Searle, Crown Buildings, 188 Fleet Street. 1872. [All rights are reserved.]

Pp. 292. 19 × 13 cm. Green cloth; front and spine lettered and decorated in gold and black. 32 pp. of advs. bound in at end, same as in *b*. Reset and printed in Great Britain, Gilbert and Rivington, Printers, London. There are variations in binding, notably one in blue cloth, with entirely different decorations, pages trimmed to 18 × 12 cm., all edges gilt, without advs. at end. An engraved frontispiece is sometimes found, apparently borrowed from some other book as it has no connection with the subject matter.

d

[Same title.] Fourth edition, with maps and additions.

[Same imprint as *a* (Boston), dated 1874.]

Pp. v + 308; 2 folding maps lithographed by Julius Bien.

Map 1. Topographical sketch of California.

Map 2. Section of the Southern Sierra Nevada showing the culminating group. Scale 6 miles to one inch.

Besides the maps, the additions consist of a preface, dated March 1874, and 17 new pages in chapter xiii, "Mount Whitney."

There are large-paper copies of this edition, of the same size and style as those mentioned under *a*.

This edition was reprinted a number of times without change in text, but designated as "Fifth," "Sixth," etc., up to "Ninth" edition. The dates observed run from 1875 to 1886, and "n.d.," with publisher's imprints "James R. Osgood & Co.," "Houghton, Osgood & Co.," "The Riverside Press," and "Ticknor & Co." There are variations in quality of paper and in color of binding cloth.

e

[Same title.] New edition, with additional chapter and two maps.

[Same imprint as *c* (London), dated 1874.]

Pp. 308; 2 folding maps (same as in *d*). The preface of *d* is not in the London edition. The binding of the observed copy is red cloth, but in other respects the same as the blue cloth copy of *c*, including the irrelevant frontispiece. (The Bancroft Library has a copy in green and gold, same as *c*, with 48 pp. of advs.)

f

[Same title.]

New York: Charles Scribner's Sons. 1902.

Pp. xi + 378; (no maps). 19 × 13 cm. Green cloth. Completely reset; a few minor changes in the text. The preface of *d* is here abridged; and there is a one-page explanatory note. This edition was reprinted from time to time, with corresponding dates on the t.p.

g

[London edition, same paging and contents as *f*.] T. Fisher Unwin, 1903, red cloth.

h

Mountaineering in the Sierra Nevada. By Clarence King. ["Altiora petimus."] Edited and with a preface by Francis P. Farquhar.
W. W. Norton & Company, Inc., Publishers. New York. [1935.]

Pp. 320; frontispiece (portrait of King) and illustrations from photographs by Ansel Adams, Cedric Wright, Marjory Bridge Farquhar, Lee L. Stopple, J. H. Czock. 22 × 15 cm. Salmon cloth.

i

[Same as *h*, reprinted September, 1946. Reset, page for page; printed on lighter-weight paper; bound in blue cloth.]

j

[Same as *i* except for imprint: Adam & Charles Black. 4, 5 & 6 Soho Square London W. 1. 1947. Printed in the United States, but bound in England. Yellow buckram, red lettering on front and spine. 1,000 copies printed.]

Clarence King (1842–1901) was born at Newport, Rhode Island. He attended the Sheffield Scientific School at Yale, 1859–1862, and in 1863 went to California with his friend James Terry Gardner. (In the earlier editions of *Mountaineering* the name is spelled Gardner, but beginning with *f* (1902) it is Gardiner to conform to the change made by the man himself during the latter part of his life.) Soon after his arrival, King met Professor William H. Brewer, Whitney's chief assistant in the California State Geological Survey. "Brewer offered him a position in the Survey and from that moment Clarence King became, first a disciple, later a master in the science of geology." (Preface to *h*.) (See also "Clarence King's First Western Journey," by David H. Dickason, in the *Huntington Library Quarterly*, November, 1943, Vol. 7, No. 1.)

King accompanied Brewer to Lassen Peak and northern California at the end of the summer of 1863, and in the summer of 1864 was with Brewer again, entering the Sierra by way of General Grant Grove and Roaring River. From a high peak which they named Mount Brewer, members of the party saw to the southwest a higher peak which they named Mount Whitney. King, with Dick Cotter, a packer, set out to try to climb this peak, but succeeded only in getting to Mount Tyndall. A short time afterward King reached Mount Whitney by another route but failed in an attempt to reach the summit.

In the winter and spring of 1865–66 King and Gardner went to Arizona to make a survey in the northwestern portion of the Territory. An account of their return journey is given in the first chapter of *Mountaineering*. During the summer of 1866 King and Gardner made a survey of the Yosemite region and climbed Mount Clark, the "Obelisk" of the "Merced Ramblings" chapter in *Mountaineering*. In that chapter there is curiously interpolated an account of his visit, in 1868, to Shoshone Falls of Snake River, Idaho, which had been published in the *Overland Monthly*, October, 1870.

Ever since his overland journey in 1863, King had been developing a plan for a survey of the route across the continent along which the Union Pacific and Central Pacific railroads were being built—roughly, the line of the 40th parallel of latitude. He spent the winter of 1866–67 in Washington, where he persuaded Congress to make an appropriation for such a survey. King, at the age of 25, was appointed Geologist-in-charge, subject to the direction of General A. A. Humphreys, Chief of Engineers, U. S. Army. Field work of the United States Geological Exploration of the Fortieth Parallel was carried on through the seasons of 1867 to 1873, after which several years were spent in producing reports and monographs. King's part in these publications is found principally in Volume I, *Systematic Geology*, published in 1878, and in the *Atlas*, 1876, although he contributed also to Volume III, *Mining Industry*, 1870, largely written by James D. Hague.

In 1879, owing in considerable measure to King's influence, Congress established the United States Geological Survey. He was appointed its first director, a position which he resigned after two years to enter private practice in the field of mining. ("The Life and Scientific Work of Clarence King," by S. F. Emmons, in the *Engineering and Mining Journal*, January 4, 1902; "Biographical Notice of Clarence King," by R. W. Raymond, in *Transactions of the American Institute of Mining Engineers*, for 1902, Vol. 33; and in contributions to *Clarence King Memoirs: The Helmet of Mambrino,* New York and London, 1904.)

It was during the period of the Fortieth Parallel Survey that the events recorded in chapters 10 to 13 of *Mountaineering in the Sierra Nevada* occurred. King appears to have parted reluctantly from the mountain regions of California, for these events have little relation to the work of his survey. In September, 1870, he ascended Mount Shasta and examined its volcanic and glacial features. Glaciers were plainly and unmistakably visible, and King hastened to send his lieutenants, Samuel F. Emmons and Arnold Hague, to Mount Rainier and Mount Hood, respectively, to see if glaciers were on those peaks, too. Glaciers suddenly seemed to be everywhere, and King made quite a show of his discovery. In an article in the *American Journal of Science and Arts* (3d Series, Vol. 1, March, 1871), "On the Discovery of Actual Glaciers in the Mountains of the Pacific Slope," he made a formal announcement, and in "Active Glaciers within the United States," *Atlantic Monthly*, March 1871, he reached another audience. As a matter of fact, glaciers had been seen and mentioned before. Dr. William Fraser Tolmie, in 1833, and Lieutenant (later General) August Valentine Kautz, in 1857, had seen glaciers on Mount Rainier, but their narratives were not published until after 1870. Yet in *Harper's New Monthly Magazine* (November, 1869, Vol. 39) there was available an article by Edmund T. Coleman, of the Alpine Club (London), "Mountaineering on the Pacific: An Ascent of Mount Baker," in which there is a convincing description of a glacier on Mount Baker. Coleman disputes at length in *The Alpine Journal* (August, 1877, Vol. 8, pp. 233–242, "Mountains and Mountaineering in the Far West") King's claim to priority in the discovery of glaciers in the United States. (See also remarks by George Davidson in *Proceedings of the California Academy of Sciences,* March 6, 1871, Vol. 4, pp. 161–162.)

It was King's glacier article in the *Atlantic Monthly,* however, that led directly to the publication of *Mountaineering in the Sierra Nevada.* The editors wanted more from this entertaining young author and King was induced to write a series of articles. In a letter dated February 24, 1871, to James T. Fields, who had just turned over his magazine and publishing business to James R. Osgood, King discussed the relative merits of proposals for a title: "Sierra Nevada Papers," "High Mountain Papers," and "Mountaineering in the Sierra Nevada." (Facsimile, with comment by Francis P. Farquhar, in *The Letters of Western Authors,* No. 10, October 1935, "Clarence King," published for its members by The Book Club of California.) The papers appeared in the *Atlantic* in 1871, as follows: "The Range," May; "Through the Forest," June; "The Ascent of Mount Tyndall," July; "The Descent of Mount Tyndall," August; "Kaweah's Run," October; "Wayside Pikes," November; and "Shasta," December. With few changes, but with some additions, these articles were gathered into the book, which appeared early in 1872. By the end of the year it had been printed in London.

In the year following its publication an event occurred which made necessary a revision of the chapter on Mount Whitney. In that chapter King had given a vivid account of his ascent of the mountain in 1871. But in *Proceedings of the California Academy of Sciences* for August 4, 1873 (Vol. 5, pp. 139–144), there appeared a communication from W. A. Goodyear which showed beyond doubt that King had been on the wrong peak. On hearing the news, King hastened to the scene and climbed the true Mount Whitney—though not before several others had preceded him. Consequently, he added seventeen pages to his chapter, and the publishers at the same time took the opportunity to insert two useful maps. This new edition, *d,* is called the "Fourth," but I have not been able to find out why. No copies marked "Second" or "Third" have been noted; so I conclude that the edition of 1872 was probably reprinted twice but without notation to that effect. The presence or absence of the publisher's monogram on the title page of some copies may have a bearing on this point. A copy dated 1872, lacking the monogram, has on verso of title page: "Electrotyped and Printed by Welch, Bigelow & Co." As this does not appear on the monogrammed copies that I have noted, it may be that the monogrammed issue is the true first edition, reprints from electrotyped plates constituting the "second" and "third." For an account of the disputes about Mount Whitney and King's part therein see "The Story of Mount Whitney," by Francis P. Farquhar (*Sierra Club Bulletin*, 1929, Vol. 14, No. 1). The latest editions, *h* and *i*, have a preface and notes that give warning of some of the exaggerations to be found in King's accounts as well as of the fictional character of several of the chapters.

The lack of further works from the pen of Clarence King has been deplored by his friends and admirers as well as by the thousands who have read *Mountaineering in the Sierra Nevada.* I have discussed this in an introduction to a reprinting, in book form, published by the Book Club of California, San Francisco, 1938, of his story "The Helmet of Mambrino." What an addition to American literature it would have been if he had written a book about his experiences in the decade after the *Mountaineering*, which would have included such episodes as the Diamond Hoax and The Three Lakes! Of the former we have only his official reports, including "Copy of Official Letter addressed November 11th, 1872, to the Board of Directors of the San Francisco and New York Mining and Commercial Company by Clarence King, Geologist in Charge, Discovering the New Diamond Fields to be a Fraud" (12 pp., no place, no date), which must be supplemented by the accounts of others, such as *The Great Diamond Hoax and Other Stirring Incidents in the Life of Asbury Harpending*, San Francisco, 1913. Of "The Three Lakes," the existence of only one copy of the three originally prepared is now known (in possession of George Gibbs, of Los Angeles); it has been reprinted, with an introduction, in the *Sierra Club Bulletin* (1939, Vol. 24, No. 3).

King's days of mountaineering in the Sierra Nevada have been appropriately commemorated by the naming of a fine peak (12,909 feet) called after him by the Brewer party of the Whitney Survey in 1864, now known as Mount Clarence King. It stands between branches of the South Fork of Kings River, close to peaks named for his associate James Terry Gardiner (or Gardner) and Dick Cotter, his companion on the Mount Tyndall adventure.

Listed in *The Zamorano Eighty*, No. 47.

13 *Lester's Yo-Semite*

The Yo-Semite; its history, its scenery, its development. By John Erastus Lester. Entered according to Act of Congress in the year 1873, by John Erastus Lester, in the office of the Librarian of Congress at Washington. Providence: Printed for the Author. 1873.

Pp. 40. Printed paper wrappers (olive). 25½ × 16 cm.

This paper is noteworthy for its appreciation of John Muir, whom the author met in Yosemite Valley. (Badè, *The Life and Letters of John Muir,* Vol. I, 1923, p. 360.) The author states that the paper was prepared for and read before the Rhode Island Historical Society, at their Cabinet, December 17, 1872, and that it was published at the request of many friends. My copy, in original wrappers, is inscribed by the author with the date "Feby. 8th, 1873." A copy in the Bancroft Library is bound in purple boards with gold title on cover, inscribed "London, 24 June 1873." Copies have been noted also in the California State Library and in the Huntington Library.

Lester also wrote a book covering more extensively his trip to the Pacific Coast: "The Atlantic to the Pacific. What to see, and how to see it. By John Erastus Lester, author of 'The Yo-Semite its history, its scenery, its development.'" (Boston: Shepard and Gill, 1873. Pp. 365, 1 p. adv.; map. Green or brick-red cloth; gilt decoration and lettering on front, gilt lettering on spine. 16½ × 11 cm. Map of the Yo-Semite Valley. Scale, 1 mile = 2 in. Also, London, 1873, blue cloth.) In his chapters on Yosemite (pp. 161–213) he mentions many of its pioneers, such as Clark, Hutchings, Lamon, John Smith of the Cosmopolitan Saloon, and Muir.

The following obituary notice appeared in the *Providence Journal* (May 5, 1900): "John Erastus Lester, aged 59 years, died Thursday after an extended illness. He was well known in this city and attained a reputation as an author and as a pomologist. By profession he was a lawyer. He was born Aug. 3, 1840, in this city, and attended the public schools of that period, graduating with honors. After leaving school he entered Brown University and was a member of the class of '62, taking the degree of A.M. On leaving Brown he took a course of study in the Harvard Law School, graduating in 1864. He studied law with C. S. Bradley. Later, ill-health compelled Mr. Lester to sever his connection with the legal profession. He travelled extensively throughout the West, and shortly afterwards wrote his first book, 'The Yosemite,' which was followed by 'From the Atlantic to the Pacific.' After completing his writings he was again taken ill and his doctors advised an European trip, at the conclusion of which he returned to this city and engaged in the practice of law. Some few years ago he was obliged to retire on account of poor health, which ultimately resulted in his death. . . ."

14 *Joseph LeConte's Ramblings*

a

A Journal of ramblings through the High Sierras of California by the "University Excursion Party."

Francis & Valentine: Commercial Printing House, 517 Clay Street, San Francisco. 1875.

Pp. 103; plates, consisting of mounted original photographs with titles and borders printed in red. 21½ × 13½ cm. The photographs are 11 × 8 cm. Bright blue cloth, gold lettering on front.

The author's name is given on the cover "Prof. Joseph LeConte." It does not appear on the title page, but the preface is signed "J. L'C."

b

Ramblings through the High Sierra. By Joseph LeConte. *Publication No. 21 of the Sierra Club*. San Francisco. 1900.

Pp. 107; 12 plates, of which one is a halftone reproduction of the frontispiece of *a*, the others from photographs by Joseph N. LeConte (son of the author). 24½ × 15½ cm. Paper wrappers (front cover constitutes title page).

Contents same as the corresponding pages of the *Sierra Club Bulletin*, January, 1900, Vol. 3, No. 1.

c

A journal of ramblings through the High Sierra of California by the University Excursion Party. Joseph LeConte.

San Francisco: The Sierra Club. 1930.

Pp. x + [6] + 152; 5 illustrations (4 of which are selected from the original edition, *a*, the other is a facsimile of the t.p. of *a*). 21½ × 14½ cm. Blue boards, linen back, printed label on spine. (Also, copies bound in heavy paper with a different printed label.)

Foreword and bibliographical notes by Francis P. Farquhar.

Joseph LeConte (1823–1901), a native of Georgia and a student of Agassiz at Harvard, came from South Carolina College to the newly established University of California in 1869 as Professor of Geology and Natural History. "At the end of the first session of the University," he writes (*The Autobigraphy of Joseph LeConte*, edited by William Dallam Armes; New York: D. Appleton and Company, 1903; p. 247), "eight of the students invited Professor Frank Soulé, Jr. and me to join them in a camping trip to the Sierras, and we joyfully accepted. The trip was almost an era in my life. We were gone six weeks and visited the Yosemite, the high Sierra, Lake Mono and the volcanoes in the vicinity, and Lake Tahoe. . . . We had no tent, but slept under trees with only the sky above us. I never enjoyed anything so much in my life—perfect health, the merry party of young men, the glorious scenery, and, above all, the magnificent opportunity for studying mountain origin and structure." This took place in July and August, 1870.

John Muir, then 32 years old (LeConte was 47), spending his second summer in the Sierra, accompanied the party to Tenaya Lake, Tuolumne Meadows, and Mount Dana. Of a memorable night at Tenaya Lake, LeConte writes: "After supper, I went with Mr. Muir and sat on a high rock jutting into the lake. It was a full moon. I never saw a more delightful scene. . . . The deep stillness of the night; the silvery light and deep shadows of the mountains; the reflection on the water, broken into thousands of glittering points by the ruffled surface; the gentle lapping of the wavelets upon the rocky shore—all these seemed exquisitely harmonized with one another and the grand harmony made answering music in our hearts. . . . For an hour we remained sitting in silent enjoyment of this delicious scene, which we reluctantly left to go to bed." (Edition *a*, p. 53; *c*, pp. 73–74.) Muir was equally impressed; in a letter to Mrs. Carr he wrote: "After moonrise LeConte and I walked to the lake-shore and climbed upon a big sofa-shaped rock that stood islet-like a little way out in the shallow water, and here we found another bounteous throne of earthly grace, and I doubt if John in Patmos saw grander visions than we." (*Letters to a Friend, Title 21*, p. 91.)

The original edition, *a,* was printed for the members of the party, ten in number. Professor LeConte's son, Joseph N. LeConte, tells me that he thinks twelve copies were made for each of them. The edition, therefore, probably consisted of about 120 copies, not 20 as stated by Cowan (Bibliography, 1914). The photograhic prints must have been procured from one or more of the professional photographers who operated in Yosemite Valley. "We here had our party photographed in costume. The photographer is none of the best, but we hope the picture will be a pleasure to our friends in Oakland." (P. 35.) The Professor does injustice to the artist, for the result, as shown in the frontispiece of the book, is remarkably good.

Most of edition *b,* reprinted by the Sierra Club in 1900 in the *Sierra Club Bulletin* and as a separate publication, was destroyed in the San Francisco fire of 1906. In 1930 the *Ramblings* was again reprinted by the club in an edition, *c,* of 1,500 copies. Although nothing can quite equal the charm of the original thin blue volume with its photographs, the 1930 edition is a very attractive book.

15 *Bunnell's Discovery of the Yosemite*

a

Discovery of the Yosemite, and the Indian War of 1851, which led to that event. By Lafayette Houghton Bunnell, M.D., of the Mariposa Battalion, one of the discoverers, late surgeon Thirty-Sixth Regiment Wisconsin Volunteers.

Chicago: Fleming H. Revell, 148 and 150 Madison Street.

On verso of title page: Entered . . . 1880. . . . Stereotyped and printed by The Chicago Legal News Company.

Pp. 331 (t.p. is p. 1); frontispiece (portrait of author), map of the Yosemite Valley (1 p.), 6 illustrations out of text, 13 illustrations in text. 19½ × 13½ cm. Green (or gray-brown, or maroon) cloth; YOSEMITE, in gold, slanting across front cover.

b

[Same title; no date.]

On verso of title page: J. L. Regan & Co., Printers and Binders, 226 & 228 Lake Street, Chicago.

Pp. 349 (t.p. is p. 1); same illustrations as *a*. 4 pp. of advs. at end. 19½ × 13½ cm. Dark brown cloth; YOSEMITE / L. H. BUNNELL, M.D.., in gold, horizontally on front cover.

The introduction has been rewritten, chiefly withdrawing apologies for the author's shortcomings. The caption under the first illustration has been changed.

From p. 13 to p. 317 the text appears to be from the original stereotyped plates. Page 318 has been rewritten. A new chapter (xx) is inserted, pp. 319–332, and the former chapter xx is expanded to two (xxi and xxii) by the addition of three pages about the big trees at the end of chapter xxi.

There is a reprint on a poorer grade of paper; 12 (or 8) pp. of advs. at end; lighter brown (or green) cloth; address of J. L. Regan & Co. is 226, 228 and 230 Lake Street.

c

[Same title.] Third edition; revised and corrected.

Fleming H. Revell Company. New York: 30 Union Square: East./ Chicago: 148 and 150 Madison St.

On verso of title page: Entered . . . 1880–1892 . . .

Pp. 1–12 (incl. t.p.); 1, 2, 2b, 3a, 3, 4, 4b, 5a, 5, 6, 6b, 7a, 7, 8, 8b, 9a, 9, 10, 10b, 11a, 11–349; frontispiece (portrait of author, new cut); map (new, double size); same illustrations, with two additions, one out of text, one in text (p. 134). No advs. 19½ × 13½ cm. Blue cloth; THE/ YOSEMITE/ L. H. BUNNELL, in gold, horizontally on front cover.

d

[Same title.] Fourth edition—reprinted from third edition, with new map and illustrations.

G. W. Gerlicher, publisher, Los Angeles, 1911.

Pp. i–xii (incl. t.p.), 1–355; frontispiece same as in *a* and *b;* folding map (19 × 36 cm.); 32 illustrations (halftones from photos by J. T. Boysen) out of text. 19 × 13½ cm. Red cloth; DISCOVERY/ OF THE/ YOSEMITE/ L. H. BUNNELL, in gold, horizontally on front cover.

A "publisher's note," p. xii, says that "no attempt at revision has been made."

Although Walker's party, in 1833, had undoubtedly looked into Yosemite Valley from the rim above, and more than one prospector in 1849 or 1850 had had a glimpse of it from some point of vantage, the effective discovery dates from March, 1851, when the Mariposa Battalion pursued Indians into the Valley. Bunnell's narrative is the principal source of information about this episode. In spite of some shortcomings as a writer, the author commands respect for the thoroughness and reliability of his history.

Lafayette Houghton Bunnell was born in Rochester, New York, March, 1824. His early life was spent in Detroit and at La Crosse, Wisconsin. He served in the Mexican War in 1847 and came to California in 1849. Bunnell did not have a systematic education in medicine, but picked up knowledge through association and experience in Detroit and in the Mexican War, so that in the Civil War he was able to serve as a hospital steward and surgeon. He received the honorary degree of Doctor of the Art of Medicine from La Crosse Medical College, October 24, 1864. After the Civil War he settled at Homer, Minnesota, where he died July 21, 1903 (See "Lafayette Houghton Bunnell, M.D., Discoverer of the Yosemite," by Howard A. Kelly, M.D., in *Annals of Medical History*, Vol. 3, No. 2, New York, 1921.)

Bunnell wrote an article for *Hutchings' California Magazine* (Vol. 3, No. 11, May, 1859, pp. 498–505) on "How the Yo-Semite Valley was Discovered and Named." Many years later he amplified the information in this article by a letter published in the *Century Magazine* (September, 1890, Vol. 40, pp. 795–797); portions of the letter omitted by *Century* were printed in *Report of the Yosemite Valley Commissioners* for 1889–90, pp. 9–13 (*Title* 23).

Another account of the Mariposa Battalion and its Yosemite experiences is in the *History of Fresno County, California* (Wallace W. Elliott & Co., publishers, San Francisco, 1881, pp. 171–181), which includes the muster roll of Companies A, B, and C, and the orders issued by Major Savage.

Cover, *Grand and Sublime Scenery of the Sierra Nevada*

16 *Elliott's Guide to the Grand and Sublime Scenery*

A guide to the grand and sublime scenery of the Sierra Nevada in the region about Mount Whitney. The object of this little work is to call the attention of our own people, as well as those who may visit us, to a comparatively unknown and unexplored region abounding in Grand Scenery, wild and unvisited by tourists. It thus affords all the pleasure to lovers of nature in all her undisturbed glory and grandeur. Hoping these imperfect pages and sketches may incite others to a thorough exploration and penciling of our Alps, is our only hope of reward. Illustrated from sketches by Wales and Eisen, and from photographs by Dusy.

Prepared and published by W. W. Elliott & Co., lithographers and engravers. 421 Montgomery St., San Francisco 1883.

Pp. 60; 15 plates (8 lithographs, 7 woodcuts); 16 cuts and 1 diagram in text; 1 map. Paper covers, ornamental printing, in brown and black on buff, front and back. 23 × 15 cm.

Guide map to the grand scenery of the Sierra Nevada. Photo-engraved from pen drawing by J. W. A. Wright for Elliott & Co., publishers, 421 Mont. St., San Francisco. Scale: Each square includes sixteen townships. 21 × 25 cm.

The description is of a copy in my collection. It contains a few pencil notes in the handwriting of F. H. Wales. Professor J. N. LeConte has a copy with more extensive notes written in by J. W. A. Wright. The only other copies I know of are: University of California Library, bound with some other pamphlets under title "Pamphlets on Yosemite, etc., Vol. I"; Library of the University of California at Los Angeles; State Library, State of New Hampshire, Concord; and California State Library, Sacramento. The covers of the last differ from those of the others: the design and wording are quite different, the printing is red and black on white, and, in addition, there is a lithographed group of four scenes entitled "Glimpses in Tehipite Valley" on the inside of the front cover; moreover, on the title page the date has apparently been altered by pen or by overprinting to "1886."

The publisher of this *Guide* had previously published a "*History of Fresno County, California,* with illustrations descriptive of its scenery, farms, residences, public buildings, factories, hotels, business houses, schools, churches, etc., from original drawings, including biographical sketches." Although my copy of this *History* is dated 1881 on the title page and 1882 on the cover, it actually includes information for the year 1883. Pages 231 to 246 of the *History* are entitled "Grand and Sublime Scenery" and contain most of the material to be found in the *Guide,* although there are some variations. The Bancroft Library copy is dated 1882 on the title page as well as on the cover; the map is dated 1883. On page 231 of the *History* is the following: "Note—It is our intention to issue this article on scenery, in a small volume, or guide book to which will be added a number of engravings and lithographs, from photographs of Frank Dusy, and sketches furnished by J. W. A. Wright, that could not be prepared in time for this article." The sketches by Wright seem not to have materialized; but there are in the *Guide* three lithographs from photographs by Dusy, two from sketches by Gustave Eisen, one from a sketch by Wales, and two others, one of which, on a larger scale, was in the *History.* The map in the *History* is dated 1883. It extends about 15 miles farther east than the one in the *Guide* and there are a few minor differences in lettering. There is also in the *Guide,* not in the *History,* a panorama of "The Sierras as seen from Hanford." This panorama was printed also in the *Mining and Scientific Press* for November 3, 1883, to accompany an article by J. W. A. Wright entitled "The Distant Sierra."

The most important additions in the *Guide* are the lithographs. Frank Dusy (1836–1898), of Fresno County, was the first to photograph the canyon of the Middle Fork of Kings River. In 1879 he carried a bulky portrait camera with all its equipment over the terrifically steep and rugged trail into Tehipite. Gustavus A. Eisen (1847–1940), Ph.D. (University of Upsala), scientist and archaeologist, managed his brother's vineyard in Fresno, 1874–1880, and visited the Sierra with Dusy. He was one of those whose activities led to the establishment of Sequoia and General Grant national parks in 1890.

The information in the latter part of the *Guide* was derived largely from a trip made by Wallace, Wales, and Wright to Mount Whitney in 1881. James William Abert Wright, a graduate of Princeton, 1857, wrote to the *San Francisco Daily Evening Post* some letters about the trip which were published in the issues of September 3, September 17, and November 3, 1881. Frederick Henry Wales (1845–1925), a native of Massachusetts, graduated from Dartmouth in 1872, and from the Hartford Theological Seminary in 1875, and lived in Tulare County for many years as a Congregational minister, editor, and farmer. Under the lithograph made from his sketch of Mount Whitney, Wales has written, in my copy of the *Guide:* "This has been altered quite a little from my original sketch." William B. Wallace (1849–1926), a native of Missouri, was a judge of the Superior Court of Tulare County, 1899–1926; he wrote an account of the trip in *Mount Whitney Club Journal* (May, 1902, Vol. I).

An account of the activities on Mount Whitney in 1881, in which Wallace, Wales, and Wright participated with the party of Samuel Pierpont Langley, of the Allegheny Observatory, will be found in "The Story of Mount Whitney," by Francis P. Farquhar (*Sierra Club Bulletin,* 1935, Vol. 20, No. 1, and 1947, Vol. 32, No. 4).

Yours ever affectionately

C. F. Gordon Cumming.

17 *Gordon-Cumming's Granite Crags*

a

Granite crags. By C. F. Gordon Cumming. Author of 'At home in Fiji,' 'Fire fountains,' 'A lady's cruise in a French man-of-war,' 'In the Hebrides.' With illustrations.

William Blackwood and Sons. Edinburgh and London. MDCCCLXXXIV.

Pp. viii + 384; 8 plates (photoengraved); map; 24 pp. of advs. 21 × 14 cm. Dark blue cloth.

Map of the Yosemite Valley. 17 × 10½ cm.

The illustrations are from drawings made by the author in 1878.

b

Granite crags of California. By C. F. Gordon Cumming. Author of [same as *a*, plus 'Wanderings in China']. With illustrations. New edition.

William Blackwood and Sons. Edinburgh and London. MDCCCLXXXVI.

Pp. viii + 384; 5 plates (autotype); map, same as in *a*. 20 × 13½ cm. Light blue cloth, ornamentation on front.

Three illustrations in *a* are omitted in *b;* the others are from the same originals, but reproduced by a different process.
The text is the same in both.

Constance Frederica Gordon-Cumming was born at Altyre, Morayshire, Scotland, May 26, 1837, and died at Crieff, Scotland, September 4, 1924. She wrote an autobiography, *Memories,* published by William Blackwood and Sons, Edinburgh and London, 1904 (pp. xii + 487; 7

photogravures and 17 other illustrations), which is the source of the following information: "My father, Sir William Gordon-Cumming, Chief of Clan Comyn or Cumming, was as splendid a Highlander as ever trod the heather, only excelled in beauty and stature by his own second son, Roualeyn, who was certainly the grandest and most beautiful human I ever beheld. . . . The spelling of surnames in ancient documents is always liable to variation, but probably no other has lent itself so largely to the fancy of the scribe." Cumeine, Commines, Cumyn, Comyn, Cummine, and the modern Cumming are among the forms cited. Her grandfather, Sir Alexander Penrose Comyn (born 1749), assumed the name of Gordon when he succeeded to the property of Gordonstoun and the double name passed to his son Sir William. The hyphen is generally but not invariably used by Miss Gordon-Cumming in *Memories,* although on the title page of that book and on that of *Granite Crags* it is omitted. In her signature, shown with a portrait, in *Memories* the writing is run together in a way that begs the question. A peculiarity of the signature requires explanation: the second name is written "Fred.[eka]," to indicate the name by which she was always known in the family—"Eka." One of her brothers, Roualeyn (1820–1866), known as "The Mighty Lion-Hunter of South Africa," wrote *Five Years of a Hunter's Life in the Far Interior of South Africa* (1850). Another brother, William (1829–1908), also a famous hunter in India, wrote *Wild Men and Wild Beasts* (1871).

In the '70s and '80s Miss Gordon-Cumming traveled far and wide throughout the world. Deeply interested in everything she saw, she wrote an almost uninterrupted series of letters to family and friends. These were published in a succession of books which included the following as well as the title under discussion: *At Home in Fiji* (2 vols., 1881); *A Lady's Cruise in a French Man-of-War* (2 vols., 1882); *Fire Fountains* (2 vols., 1883); *In the Himalayas and on the Indian Plains* (1884); *Wanderings in China* (2 vols., 1886); *Two Happy Years in Ceylon* (2 vols., 1892). She was also a prolific writer for magazines; a list of her articles in *Memories* includes: "The World's Wonderlands" (Wyoming and New Zealand), in the *Overland Monthly* (January, 1885); "Earth's

Boiling Fountains," in *Atalanta* (February, March, 1888); and "Destruction of the American Bison," in *Good Words* (June, 1884). In the course of her travels she climbed Fujiyama, in Japan, and Adam's Peak, in Ceylon.

Her visit to Yosemite followed soon after her arrival in San Francisco from Tahiti in April, 1878. It was her intention to "do" the valley in a few days, but as soon as she saw it she sent word to cancel a passage booked for Honolulu and settled down for a stay of nearly three months. She visited all the accessible points in and around the valley, including Clouds Rest and Sentinel Dome, became acquainted with the permanent inhabitants and with many of the visitors, read acquisitively the works of Whitney, Hutchings, and other writers on Yosemite and on California, sketched, painted, and wrote the fluent, gracious letters that were gathered into *Granite Crags*. Several of her water colors are now in the Yosemite Museum. Before her return to San Francisco she visited the Calaveras Grove—she had earlier seen the Mariposa Grove on her way to Yosemite. She mentions the bark of "The Mother of the Forest" that was taken to the Crystal Palace at Sydenham, "where it was unfortunately destroyed in the great fire." (See *Title* 3.) Of the tree itself she says: "I can see her from where I now sit—a ghastly object—her sides still transfixed with wooden implements of torture—the St. Sebastian of the forest." She also made the uncommon excursion, by horseback, to the South Calaveras Grove, of which she wrote an appreciative description.

18 *Hutchings' In the Heart of the Sierras*

a

In the heart of the Sierras. The Yo Semite Valley, both historical and descriptive: and scenes by the way. Big tree groves. The High Sierra, with its magnificent scenery, ancient and modern glaciers, and other objects of interest; with tables of distances and altitudes, maps, etc. Profusely illustrated. By J. M. Hutchings, of Yo Semite.

Published at the Old Cabin, Yo Semite Valley, and at Pacific Press Publishing House, Oakland, Cal. 1886.

Frontispiece, t.p., portrait, dedication, pp. i–xii, map 1, map 2 (folded), pp. 13–496; 152 illustrations, of which 121 are cuts in text. 21½ × 15½ cm. Tan cloth; designs and lettering stamped in black and gold on front and spine.

Illustrations not in text: frontispiece—Yo Semite Valley, Cal., phototype of Gutekunst, Phila.; portrait of author—photo-typo by Britton & Rey, S.F., from photo by Thos. Houseworth, signed "Ever faithfully yours, J. M. Hutchings"; 20 photo-typos by Britton & Rey; 2 artotypes by E. Bierstadt; 1 by Heliotype P't'g. Co., Boston; 1 printed in red (snow plant); 3 line engravings; 2 maps; a total of 31.

Map 1. Map of routes to Yo Semite Valley. 10 × 16½ cm. Map 2. By permission from Topographical map of the Yosemite Valley and Vicinity. U. S. Geographical Surveys West of the 100th Meridian. Expeditions of 1878–79 under command of Capt. Geo. M. Wheeler, Corps of Engineers, U. S. Army. Part of East Central California. From topographical plat by Lt. Macomb, Nov. 30, 1883. Preliminary edition. Julius Bien & Co. Photo. lith; Heliotype Printing Co. Boston. 1: 42240. 32½ × 48 cm.

A canvasser's sample, in Yosemite Museum, contains the following: "In the Press, and will be Published about May 20th, 1886. Nearly 400 pp. of letter-press. Over 140 engravings, some 40 being full page size, about 20 of which are produced directly from the negative by the new and beautiful process of photo-lithography." The following bindings are offered: fine English cloth, embossed in jet and gold; same, gilt edges; full sheep, library style, marbled edges; half morocco, gilt edges, extra finish; full turkey morocco, gilt edges.

Distinguishing features of what appears to be the first issue are: the portrait in photo-typo by B. & R.; the frontispiece phototype by Gutekunst, in which there is no one seated behind the horse and in which the cabin has no lean-to; the presence of 2 artotypes by E. Bierstadt and the plate of Hutchings' Old Cabin by Heliotype P't'g Co. These are all in the canvasser's sample as well as in the type copy described above.

b

[Same title, imprint, and text.]

Differs from *a* in some of the illustrations. There are a few changes in the list of illustrations on pp. ix–xii. In the copies examined there are several illustrations outside of text not listed. After examining a number of copies with minor variations, I am unable to establish a standard collation; accordingly, all copies that do not have the distinguishing features of *a* are classified as *b*.

A sample collation of illustrations not in text is given as follows: frontispiece—Yo Semite Valley, Cal., photo-typo by Britton & Rey, S.F., in which someone is seated behind the horse and in which a lean-to is shown added to the cabin; portrait of author is engraved; 24 photo-typos, all by B. & R.; 1 in red and 3 line engravings, as in *a;* 2 maps; a total of 32. (In some copies the photo-typo described here as a frontispiece is found opposite p. 13.) Map 2 shows "Copied by permission" instead of "By permission from," and Photo. Lith. Britton & Rey, S.F.

The binding is usually olive cloth, designs and lettering stamped in brown and gold on front and spine (sometimes black and gold), with a bear blind-stamped on back. I have a copy in full turkey morocco, 23 × 17 cm.

c

[Same title and text as *a* and *b*.]

W. H. Thompson & Co., Boston, Mass., and Pacific Press Publishing House, Oakland, Cal. 1887.

In all respects except the imprint and date this appears to be the same as *b*. The copy described is in Boston Public Library.

d

[Same title, text, and imprint, except date, as *a* and *b*.] Date: 1888.

The principal differences are a new frontispiece and changes in the list of illustrations, 154 in all, of which 27, besides frontispiece, are photo-typos by B. & R. The frontispiece, entitled "In the Heart of the Sierras," is a photo-typo by B. & R. from a painting by C. D. Robinson.

The binding is usually olive cloth, same as *b*, all edges gilt. 22½ × 16½ cm.

I have seen a copy with the map described as in *a*, which indicates that maps left over from the first issue were used later.

e

[Same title with addition of] Tourists' Edition. A guide to California's natural attractions. More than one hundred illustrations.
Pacific Press Publishing Company, Oakland, Cal., New York, San Francisco, and London, Eng. [N.d.]

Frontispiece is composed of 4 cuts, "In the Yo Semite Valley"; pages same as in *a;* illustrations and maps are fewer and cheaper; portrait of author same as in *b*. Printed paper wrappers.

Advertisements in back refer to a "Fourth Edition" of the "Standard Edition."

With the termination of *Hutchings' California Magazine* and the publication of *Scenes of Wonder and Curiosity* (*Title 4*), James M. Hutchings entered into a long period of close association with Yosemite Valley. His adoption of the appellation, "Hutchings, of Yo Semite," seems justified, for more than anyone else he became for several decades the dominant figure in the valley. His pioneer publicizing of the valley for tourist travel, his demonstration of its habitability in winter, his ventures in hotel proprietorship, his stubborn efforts to obtain title to land and to receive compensation for his claims (see *Title* 23), are set forth in the book that crowned his publishing career—*In the Heart of the Sierras.* It contains a great deal more, however, than an account of Hutchings' personal experiences; it covers more fully than any other work of its day every aspect of Yosemite Valley and the Big Trees that could be considered of general interest to visitors. The illustrations are the finest that could be procured at the time. Although the author still drew heavily upon his old cuts from the magazine, he added a number of full-page plates, made from photographs by new processes, called "photo-typos" or "artotypes." Altogether, it lives up very well to the testimonials quoted in the advertising circulars, of which an example is as follows: " 'The illustrations, the text, the whole atmosphere of the volume, are worthy of their great subject, the Yo Semite. What can I say more?'—Rev. Joseph Cook, Boston, Mass."

Certain distinguishing marks of what I believe to be the first issue are set forth in the description under *a*. The priority of the black-and-gold over the brown-and-gold stamping on the cover is further established by the Preface, in which it is stated that "The designs for the embossed covers, in black and gold, are by Mr. Thomas Hill, the eminent and well-known California artist." However, this alone is not a sure sign of the first issue; the other features must also be present. Although I have nothing in the way of proof, it is my conjecture that Hutchings shopped around to find suitable means of reproduction for his photographic illustrations, and that after obtaining a few from Gutekunst, Bierstadt, and the Heliotype Co., he found that he could do better by concentrating the work with the San Francisco firm of Britton & Rey.

Besides his two major works, *Scenes of Wonder and Curiosity* (*Title 4*) and *In the Heart of the Sierras,* several other Yosemite publications are credited to Hutchings. "The Yo-Semite Almanac, adapted to California, Nevada, Oregon, Washington, Idaho, Montana and Utah. 1867," contains a number of intersting woodcuts, but only two are of Yosemite. It was "entered" in 1866, so there may have been an issue for that year, but the 1867 issue is the only one I have seen. Ten years later there was published by A. Roman & Co., San Francisco, "Hutchings' Tourist's Guide to the Yo Semite Valley and the Big Tree Groves for the Spring and Summer of 1877," 102 pages and one woodcut, pocket size, black cloth. In 1895 Hutchings published a "Souvenir of California. Yo Semite Valley and the Big Trees. What to See and How to See It," 102 pages, numerous illustrations from photographs, red cloth (or stiff paper) covers, pocket size. Publication was continued for two or three years, with some changes in text and illustrations and the addition of advertisements front and back.

Hutchings' name appears frequently in the literature of Yosemite. He pioneered in the development of tourist travel to the valley and was among the first to visit it in winter; he kept a hotel there; he tried in vain to establish claims to land; he fought in the Legislature and in Congress for compensation; he served from 1880 to 1884 as the Guardian of Yosemite Valley and the Mariposa Big Tree Grove (see *Title 23,* reports for those years). He was also John Muir's employer for a time, and he is pictured in *Zanita* (*Title 11*) as "Naunton." Hutchings was an energetic explorer of the High Sierra in the 1870s: he climbed many of the points around Yosemite, ascended Mount Lyell and Mount Dana, visited Muir Gorge in Tuolumne Canyon, and, in 1875, conducted a party to Kings River Canyon and to the summit of Mount Whitney. A mountain on the divide between the Middle and South forks of Kings River bears the name Mount Hutchings.

The *San Francisco Chronicle,* November 2, 1902, contained a dispatch from Yosemite from which the following paragraphs are quoted:

J. M. Hutchings, known to thousands as the father of Yosemite, met with a tragic death last evening [October 31] on the Oak-Flat grade about 500 yards above where that road intersects the floor of the valley. Having retired from the management of the Calaveras big trees and hotel, Hutchings and his wife were on their way to San Francisco, via the Yosemite. They intended to remain here a week or more and were prepared to camp out.

Yesterday morning they left Crockers and arrived at Gentry's at the point where the grade begins its zig-zag descent into the great gorge, about 3:15 o'clock in the afternoon. They had passed most of the dangerous points and had reached a quite level stretch within 500 yards of the foot. Hutchings remarked to his wife that he had never seen the valley look so beautiful in its wonderful autumn coloring. Either the grandeur of the scene caused him to relax his vigilance or the almost level part of the road made him loosen a little on the lines of the team. Mrs. Hutchings says that one of the horses shied at a large rock above the road, jumped over the wagon tongue and then started to run. Mr. Hutchings told her the team was beyond control.

They had gone but a few yards when the wagon struck the side of a large rock and Mrs. Hutchings was thrown from the wagon. About twenty feet further down Mr. Hutchings was thrown head first upon a pile of rocks and expired within five minutes. "I am very much hurt," were the only words he uttered, and when Mrs. Hutchings reached him a moment later he recognized her and then passed over the last divide.

James Mason Hutchings is buried in the cemetery in Yosemite Valley beside his first wife and his daughter Florence, who was the first white child born in the Valley and for whom Mount Florence, in Yosemite National Park, is named.

19 *Jordan's Alps of the King[s]-Kern Divide*

a

California and the Californians and the Alps of the King-Kern Divide. By David Starr Jordan, President of Leland Stanford Junior University. [Publisher's device.] New edition.

San Francisco: The Whitaker-Ray Company, Incorporated. 1903.

Pp. 63 (t.p. is p. 1); portrait (frontispiece), and 12 plates, of which 6 (from photos by J. N. LeConte) pertain to "The Alps of the King-Kern Divide." 22½ × 14½ cm. Maroon boards, cloth back, printed paper label. "The Alps of the King-Kern Divide" constitutes pp. 43–63.

b

The Alps of the King-Kern Divide. By David Starr Jordan, President of Stanford University.

San Francisco. A. M. Robertson. 1907.

Pp. 22 (h.t. is p. 1); 6 illustrations from photos by J. N. LeConte. 17½ × 12 cm. Green boards.

Jordan's article on the Kings-Kern Divide was first printed in *The Land of Sunshine,* Los Angeles (March, 1900, Vol. 12, No. 4). The 1903 edition is its first appearance in book form. "New edition" refers only to the essay, "California and the Californians," first printed in the *Atlantic Monthly* (November, 1898), and published separately in 1899 by the Whitaker-Ray Company, and again, separately, in 1907, by A. M. Robertson, San Francisco. Jordan also wrote an article, similar in character, for *Sunset,* "The Kings River Canyon and the Alps of the Great Divide" (April, 1900, Vol. 4, No. 6). These articles were inspired by a camping trip to the headwaters of the Kings in August, 1899, described by Vernon L. Kellogg, in "A Stanford Party in the Kings River Canyon," *Sunset* (November, 1899, Vol. 4, No. 1). Jordan also provided some notes and a "Sketch Map of Ouzel Basin or the East Basin of Mount Brewer" for the *Sierra Club Bulletin* (January, 1900. Vol. 3, No. 1, pp. 109–111).

The title should read "Kings-Kern," not "King-Kern." It refers to the divide between the Kings River and the Kern River. There was prevalent for a time a notion that the name of the river was "King's" or "King." Actually, it is a translation from the Spanish *Rio de los Santos Reyes* (River of the Holy Kings) and is therefore plural.

David Starr Jordan [1851–1931] was President of Stanford University 1891–1913, Chancellor 1913–1916, and after that Chancellor Emeritus. In his autobiography, *The Days of a Man* (2 vols., 1922) he speaks of the camping trip of 1899 with Professor and Mrs. Ellwood P. Cubberley and Professor Vernon L. Kellogg and others (Vol. I, pp. 648–655).

A Stanford professor, Bolton Coit Brown, in 1895, named the highest peak of the Palisades (14,254 ft.) "Mount Jordan," but the name "North Palisade" had previously been established and has been retained. However, most appropriately, a peak on the Kings-Kern Divide was named by the Sierra Club in 1925 in honor of President Jordan. (*Place Names of the High Sierra,* by Francis P. Farquhar, Sierra Club, 1926, pp. 49–50).

20 *Stewart Edward White's The Pass*

a

The Pass. By Stewart Edward White. Author of "The Blazed Trail," "The Forest," "The Mountains," etc., etc. Frontispiece in color by Fernand Lungren and many other illustrations from photographs. [Publisher's device.]

New York. The Outing Publishing Company. 1906.

Pp. viii + 198; frontispiece in color; 13 halftones; sketch map; small ornamental sketch on a lower corner of each page. 20½ × 14 cm. Blue cloth, buff lettering; mountain trail scene on front cover in light and dark blue and buff.

b

[Same title.]

Garden City, New York. Doubleday, Page & Company, 1912.

Same paging and text, same size. Olive green cloth, yellow lettering; mountain trail scene in gray, black, and green.

This is an account of an actual trip in the Sierra made in 1905 by Stewart Edward White and his wife Elizabeth, who, in the story, is called "Billy." "Wes" White, who accompanied them, was not related to the author. The Forest Ranger, not named in the book, was modeled upon Sam L. N. Ellis, of Tulare County. The White party camped at Roaring River and explored Deadman and Cloud ("Cloudy" in the book) canyons. From the head of the former they took their stock across the divide into Lone Pine Meadow on the Middle Fork of the Kaweah. The name "Elizabeth Pass," given by Stewart Edward White for his wife, has been retained for the route now followed by the trail, a little to the west of the point crossed by the 1905 party. (*Place Names of the High Sierra,* by Francis P. Farquhar, Sierra Club, San Francisco, 1926, pp. 14, 19, 24; *Guide to the John Muir Trail and the High Sierra Region,* by Walter A. Starr, Jr., Sierra Club, San Francisco, 1934, pp. 123, 124, and second edition, 1943, pp. 108, 123, 124.)

"The Pass" first appeared as a story in *The Outing Magazine* (March, April, and May, 1906). There are 22 illustrations from photographs, of which 13 were used in the book.

Stewart Edward White (1873–1946) wrote several other books descriptive of features of the Sierra Nevada, notably: *The Mountains* (New York: McClure, Phillips & Company, 1904), first printed in *The Outlook* (June to September, 1904), and *The Cabin* (Garden City, New York: Doubleday, Page & Company, 1911). He was born in Michigan, graduated from the University of Michigan in 1895 (M.A., 1903), and attended the Columbia Law School, 1896–97. He married Elizabeth Grant in 1904 and lived for a time in Santa Barbara and the latter part of his life in San Mateo, California.

21 *John Muir's Letters to a Friend*

Letters to a Friend. Written to Mrs. Ezra S. Carr. 1866–1879. By John Muir.

Boston and New York. Houghton Mifflin Company. The Riverside Press, Cambridge. 1915.

On verso of title page: Copyright, 1915, by Wanda Muir Hanna. All rights reserved. This edition consists of 300 copies.

Pp.—Prefatory Note (1 p.), 1–194. 21 × 14 cm. Dark green boards, printed paper label on spine.

Mrs. Jeanne C. (Smith) Carr, wife of Professor Ezra Slocum Carr, to whom these letters were written, had a great influence upon Muir's career. Mrs. Linnie Marsh Wolfe, in *Son of the Wilderness: The Life of John Muir* (New York: Alfred A. Knopf, 1945) says: "More than anyone else who came into John Muir's early life she became his teacher in the humanities. She formed the bridge between the crabbed isolation of his boyhood and the world of men he would have to live in. By her unfailing tact and faith in his genius she directed his aims and helped fit him for leadership." (P. 79.) Muir first knew the Carrs when he was attending the University of Wisconsin. They came to California shortly after he did and the friendship continued almost to the end of his life.

The earlier letters in this collection were written before Muir came to California. In the others, written between 1868 and 1879, Yosemite is almost constantly the theme. There are references to Hutchings, Professor LeConte, Mrs. Yelverton, Professor Kneeland, and others who visited Yosemite or wrote about it. In these letters Muir first stated his ideas about the influence of ice in the formation of Yosemite. "I believe that ice was the agent by which all of the present rocks receive their special forms." (P.156.) His approach to natural science is summarized on the next page: "Patient observation and constant brooding above the rocks, lying upon them for years as the ice did, is the way to arrive at the truths which are graven so lavishly upon them." A substantial portion of the letters in this volume was included a few years later in *The Life and Letters of John Muir,* by William Frederic Badè (Boston and New York: Houghton Mifflin Company, 2 vols., Vol. 1, 1923; Vol. 2, 1924).

William E. Colby, attorney-at-law, San Francisco, for many years Secretary of the Sierra Club, and one of Muir's closest friends, has supplied the following statement of facts that led to publication of the letters:

"When Mrs. Carr died the wonderful series of letters which John Muir had written her were inherited by her son, who sold them to George Wharton James. Muir evidently tried to get possession of these letters, but did not succeed, and, finding that they had been acquired by James, borrowed them and had them copied before returning them. His object in copying them was to use the material in preparing future publications. After his death his heirs either were advised or suspected that James would publish these letters. Therefore, Dr. William Frederic Badè, who was selected by John Muir's daughters as literary executor of the material that he had left in the form of notes, articles, and letters, hastily edited this volume of letters and published them with copyright. James was meanwhile advised that if he attempted any publication of the letters the heirs would seek an injunction to prevent him. This action would, of course, be based on the legal principle that, while the recipient and the successors in interest own the actual letters themselves, the right of publication of the material remains with the writer and his heirs and successors."

A comprehensive, although not quite complete, "Bibliography of John Muir," by Jennie Elliot Doran, appeared in the *Sierra Club Bulletin* in a number (1916, Vol. 10, No. 1) given over entirely to appreciation of Muir, who had been President of the Sierra Club from its organization in 1892 until his death on December 24, 1914. Besides the *Life and Letters* and

Son of the Wilderness, mentioned above, there have been published since 1916 two important books of Muir's writings; *Steep Trails: California, Utah, Nevada, Washington, Oregon, The Grand Cañon* (Boston and New York: Houghton Mifflin and Company, 1918); and *John of the Mountains: The Unpublished Journals of John Muir,"* edited by Linnie Marsh Wolfe (Boston: Houghton Mifflin Company, 1938). Of the earlier works, the most important relating to Yosemite and the Sierra Nevada are: *The Mountains of California* (New York: The Century Company, 1894); *Our National Parks* (Boston and New York: Houghton Mifflin and Company, 1901); *My First Summer in the Sierra* (Boston and New York, Houghton Mifflin Company, 1911); *The Yosemite* (New York: The Century Co., 1912). In addition to these books there should be mentioned: "Studies in the Sierra," a series of seven articles first published in the *Overland Monthly* (May, June, July, August, November, December, 1874, and January 1875, in Vols. 12, 13, and 14), reprinted in the *Sierra Club Bulletin* (1915–1921, in Vols. 9, 10, and 11); and several chapters in *Picturesque California and the Region West of the Rocky Mountains, from Alaska to Mexico,* edited by John Muir (New York and San Francisco: J. Dewing Publishing Company, 1888, 2 vols.). Among the most influential of Muir's magazine articles were: "The Treasures of the Yosemite," "Features of the Proposed Yosemite National Park," and "A Rival of the Yosemite (*Century Magazine,* August, 1890, September, 1890, and November, 1891, respectively). For a more contemporaneous feeling than one gets by reading Muir in the final form of his books one should turn to these *Century* articles and to the earlier ones in the *Overland Monthly* (1872–1875), *Harper's New Monthly Magazine* (1875–1878), and *Scribner's Monthly* (1878–1881), and to later articles in the *Atlantic Monthly* (1897–1913).

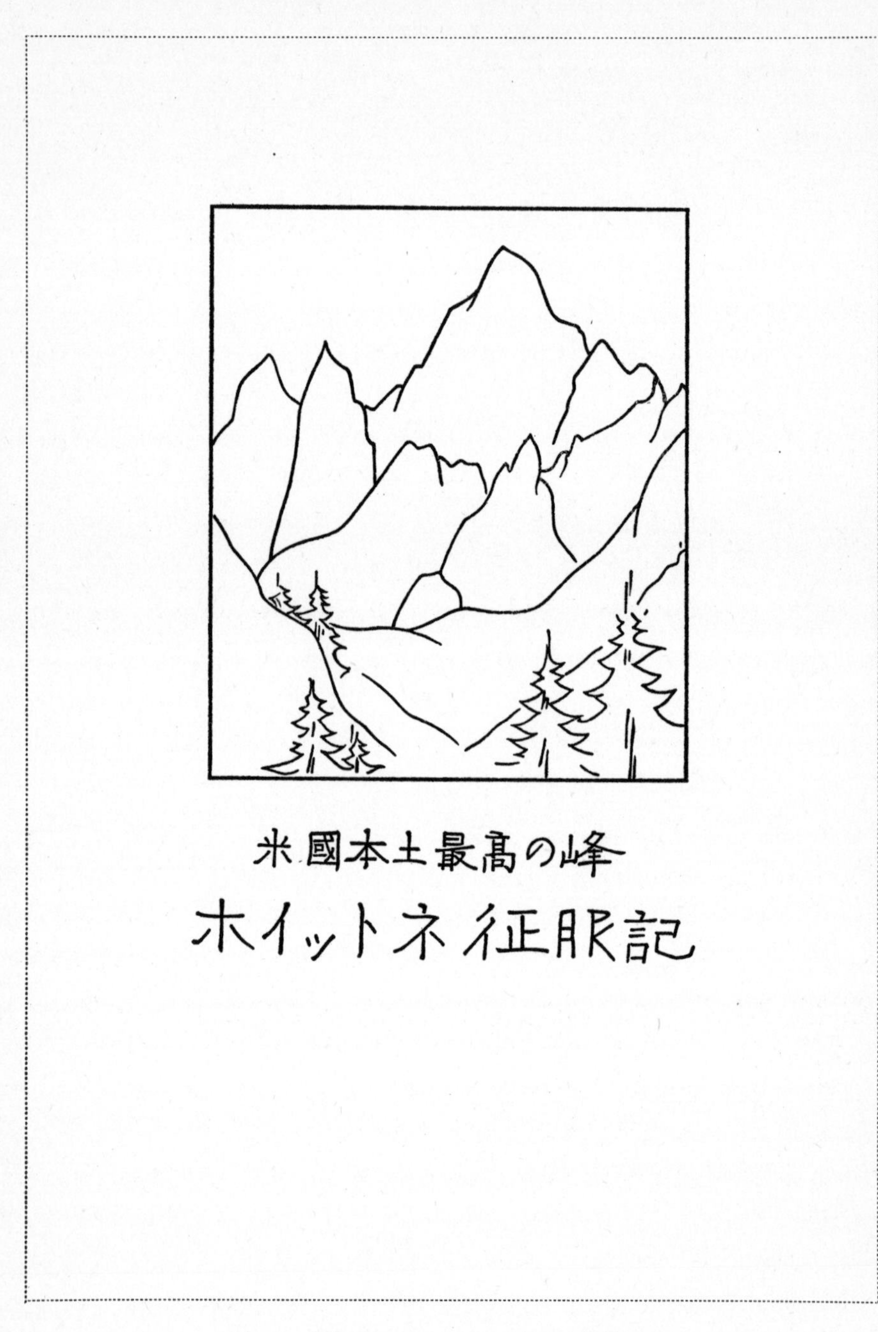

Cover, *The Conquest of Mount Whitney*

22 *Japanese Conquest of Mount Whitney*

[The conquest of Mount Whitney. By Shuki Nakamura. Tokio, 1931.]

T.p.; 13 plates containing 19 halftone illustrations from photographs; sketch map, 8½ × 8 cm., showing route from Lone Pine to Mount Whitney and return, with names in Japanese; pp. 1–5, 1–8, [1]–[2], [1]–174, colophon. 18½ × 12½ cm. Blue cloth; gold design and Japanese lettering on front (back to us) cover; gold Japanese lettering on spine. Book reads Japanese-style, from right to left.

In 1931 the author of this book was living in Los Angeles. In presenting a copy of the book to me Mr. Nakamura very kindly supplied a summary of its contents, from which the following outline of the book has been taken:

"First Chapter: To the foot of the Mountain. 1—Mount Whitney; 2—Sierra Nevada Mountain; 3—Plan of Ascent; 4—Scenery of Southern California; 5—Start Los Angeles; 6—Railway in desert; 7—Owens Lake; 8—Lone Pine. Second Chapter: Climbing. 1—Preparation; 2—Climbing; 3—Camp at Cottonwood Lake; 4—Mount Langley; 5—Sequoia National Park; 6—Largest Living thing; 7—Camping under tree. Third Chapter: At Summit. 1—To Whitney Pass; 2—Conquest of Summit. Fourth Chapter: Descend. 1—Camp at Mirror Lake; 2—Out mountain; 3—Course table; 4—Reference Book; 5—Expenditure. End."

A few details of the outline are selected, as follows:

"Plan of Ascent:—Is there permanency in Japanese Alpinism? international Alpinism, communication with guide, prepare for ascent."

"Owens Lake:—location of Valley, and size, disappointed as to lake, Los Angeles Aqueduct, world large aqueducts in ancient and modern times, Hollywood actress uses snow melting water of Sierra Nevada Mountain."

"Camping under tree:—arrival of Crabtree, moral of American alpinist is high, golden trout, Mt. Whitney at sunset, Camp fire, If there is radio we can hear music of cities, Constellation of Orion."

"Conquest of Summit:—First Japanese ascent, view on top. Alpinism, Divide of Oriental and occidental civilization, American exclusion of oriental people, great stage of the Pacific era, resolution of Japanese, Sierra Club's registration box, Sierra Club Bulletin, Smithsonian Institution its origin and activities, small house of Smithsonian Institution at top."

"Camp at Mirror Lake:—from granite High Sierra to forest zone, note camping under tree without tent, forest fire, ants & camping, big wind, storm and thunder."

"Out mountain:—Lone Pine Trail, grand view than Yosemite, met American Boy at Lone Pine station who does not understand Alpinism."

There were three in the party besides the guide—Mr. Nakamura was accompanied by Mr. T. H. Kinoshita and Mr. Yoneo Sakai. The illustrations include photographs of them standing triumphantly beside the summit cairn.

Another book, on a more ambitious plan, entitled *Record of the American Alps*, by Mr. Nakamura's companion, T. H. Kinoshita, was also published in Tokio in 1931. It is dedicated to Ojima Torimizu, "the John Muir of Japan." In addition to preliminaries, it contains 213 pages and a colophon, a folding panorama of the Sierra from Owens Valley, 4 plates in color, 88 halftones, several cuts in text, a map of Sequoia National Park with lettering in Japanese (20½ × 25 cm.), and two other maps, size 8½ × 12½ cm.; bound in green cloth, gold Japanese lettering on spine. Pages 79–195 seem to carry an account of the Mount Whitney trip, but I do not have the advantage of a key to its contents such as I have for Mr. Nakamura's book. One may learn much, however, from the illustrations, which include a statuesque portrait of Mr. Kinoshita and Mr. Sakai at the summit.

A companion volume to these books is *The National Parks of the United States* by Shuki Nakamura (Tokio, 1932).

23 *Reports of the Yosemite Valley Commissioners*

Report of the Commissioners to Manage the Yosemite Valley and the Mariposa Big Tree Grove. For the years [———]

Sacramento: Superintendent State Printing. [Year]

There are a few variations in the title, for instance: "Biennial Report," "Report of the Yosemite Commissioners."

Contained in Appendix to the Journals of the Senate and Assembly; also, for most years, issued separately, with printed paper wrappers or bound in black or dark blue cloth. Approximately 23 × 15 cm.

Nineteen numbers, as follows:

1866–67, pp. 24, including laws
1868–69, pp. 8, including memorial of J. C. Lamon
1870–71, pp. 5
1872–73, pp. 6
1874–75, pp. 17
1876–77, pp. 17
1878–79, pp. 6
1880, pp. 10
1880–1882 (April 19, 1880, to Dec. 18, 1882), pp. 29
1883–84, pp. 32
1885–86, pp. 35, including report of Wm. Ham Hall, State Engineer, dated May, 1882
1887–88, pp. 24, sketch map of Valley
1889–90, pp. 41
1891–92, pp. 28, 8 plates
1893–94, pp. 31, 4 plates
1895–96, pp. 35, 4 plates
1897–98, pp. 29
[1899–1900, none printed]
1901–02, pp. 14
1903–04, pp. 16

The first 11 pp. of the report for 1866–67 were also printed separately in 14 pp., with printed paper wrappers, San Francisco: Towne and Bacon, 1868. This report is signed J. D. Whitney, Chairman of Executive Committee, and was probably reprinted for Whitney or for the State Geological Survey.

In his book *In the Heart of the Sierras* (*Title 18*, p. 149), Hutchings writes: "The Hon. John Conness, U. S. Senator for California, in concert with I. W. Raymond and others, conceived a plan for the cession by Congress, of the Yo Semite Valley, and its more immediate surroundings, with the Mariposa Big Tree Grove, to the State of California, for the

REPORT

OF THE

COMMISSIONERS TO MANAGE

THE

YOSEMITE VALLEY

AND THE

Mariposa Big Tree Grove,

For the Years 1866-7.

SAN FRANCISCO:
TOWNE AND BACON.
1868.

Title page, *Report of the Commissioners*

purpose of setting them apart, and protecting them as public parks." Senator Conness introduced a bill in the Senate, which was promptly passed by both branches of Congress and was approved by President Lincoln on June 30, 1864. (Chapter 184 of the Statutes at Large, passed at the 30th Congress, Session 1.) The act contains the stipulation: "The State shall accept this grant upon the express condition that the premises shall be held for public use, resort, and recreation." The act further provides that the premises "be managed by the Governor of the State with eight other Commissioners, to be appointed by the Executive of California." On September 28, 1864, Governor Frederick F. Low issued a proclamation in which he appointed the Commissioners and warned and commanded all persons to desist from trespassing or settling upon the territory. Among those appointed were Professor J. D. Whitney, Galen Clark, I. W. Raymond, and Frederick Law Olmsted. An Act of Acceptance, passed at the next session of the Legislature, was approved April 2, 1866. (Chapter 536 of the Statutes of California, passed at the 16th Session of the Legislature, 1865–66.)

The consequences of this legislation were far-reaching. Out of it developed many of the policies that characterize our National Parks system, policies still in process of evolution. Through the Commissioners' reports may be traced the struggle over the subordination of private advantage to the public interest, and the constant threat of artificial encroachment upon unique scenic features and even of their destruction. At the very outset there was initiated a lawsuit over the claims of Hutchings and others to private ownership, a suit that was decided in favor of the public by the Supreme Court of California in 1871: *Low et al.* v. *Hutchings,* 41 Cal. 634. The judgment was affirmed in 1872 by the United States Supreme Court: "The Yosemite Valley Case," *Hutchings* v. *Low,* 15 Wall. (U.S.) 77.

Preservation v. *Improvement* provoked an even greater controversy, in which no Supreme Court was available for settlement. In 1882, there was published a report by Wm. Ham. Hall, State Engineer, entitled "To preserve from defacement and promote the use of the Yosemite

No.

IN THE

Supreme Court of the State of California.

F. F. LOW, Governor, and others, Commissioners, &c.,
APPELLANTS.

v.

J. M. HUTCHINGS,
DEFENDANT AND RESPONDENT.

BRIEF OF RESPONDENT.

I.

THE plaintiffs, by the Act of the Legislature of the State of California, entitled "An Act to accept the grant by the United States Government to the State of California of the Yosemite Valley," etc., were constituted the special agents of the State, "to manage and administer the grant made," and were clothed with certain powers to that end, among which is the power to "sue and be sued."

Page 1, Low v. Hutchings

Valley" (Sacramento: State Office, pp. 30). It was reprinted in the Commissioners' *Report* for 1885–86. Some of the problems discussed therein are still unsolved. To the archaeologist of the future these reports may serve as a clue to many a curious bit of masonry or overgrown road, and to the unfinished trail on the north side of the river below Vernal Fall.

As time went on, the management of Yosemite by the State Commissioners began to draw strong criticism from John Muir, Robert Underwood Johnson, and from others. (*Century Magazine,* January, 1890; *Remembered Yesterdays,* by Robert Underwood Johnson, Boston, 1923.) There was an investigation by the Legislature; the proceedings were published: "In the matter of the investigation of the Yosemite Valley Commissioners" (Senate, 1889, 40 pp., and Assembly, 1889, 430 pp). A comment upon this in the Report for 1889–90 was: "In noting these attacks we propose no defense, for none is necessary. The State's defense is in the bad character, or despicable motive or rank antecedents of her accusers." Most of the report, however, is taken up with defense. Perhaps the situation was best summed up by George Davidson, of the U. S. Coast and Geodetic Survey, in a letter printed in the same report: "I found great discordance of views in the valley; and it was evident that strong personal feelings clouded unprofessional opinions."

Hall, in his report of 1882, had recommended that the upper portions of the Merced basin be added to the grant of the Yosemite Valley in order to protect the water supply from damage by excessive cutting of timber and by the overgrazing of sheep. This was repeatedly advocated by the Commissioners. But when, at length, in 1890, Congress established Yosemite National Park, the territory was placed in the hands of a Federal rather than a State agency. Thus was created the anomaly of a state park enfolded in the very heart of a national park. This continued for fifteen years, when, after a long and bitter fight, the Legislature of California, by an act approved March 2, 1905, receded and regranted the Yosemite Valley to the United States of America. On the following day a joint resolution of the Senate and House purported to accept the recession, but the Commissioners, reluctant to give up their domain, found fault with the form of the resolution and stood fast. Finally, on June 11, 1906, Congressional action was completed, and the State Commissioners reluctantly withdrew in favor of the Federal Government. The fight over recession is decribed by William E. Colby in "Yosemite and the Sierra Club" (*Sierra Club Bulletin,* 1938, Vol. 23, No. 2, pp. 11–19), and by Linnie Marsh Wolfe in *Son of the Wilderness* (New York, 1945, pp. 301–304.)

Complete collections of these reports are seldom found. Besides my own, there is one in the California State Library, and there are nearly complete collections in the Yosemite Museum and the Bancroft Library.

24 *Reports of the Superintendents of Yosemite National Park*

Report of the Acting Superintendent of the Yosemite National Park to the Secretary of the Interior. [Year]

Washington: Government Printing Office. [Year]

(Variations in title: for 1898, "Report of the Acting Superintendents," etc.; for 1915, "Report of the Superintendent," etc.)

Included in annual reports of the Secretary of the Interior; also issued separately with printed paper wrappers. Approximately 23 × 15 cm.

Twenty-five numbers, as follows:

1891, pp. 10
1892, pp. 7
1893, pp. 9
1894, pp. 6
1895, pp. 6, Map (1)
1896, pp. 11
1897, pp. 8, Map (2)
1898, pp. 11, Map (2)
1899, pp. 7
1900, pp. 4, Map (3)
1901, pp. 6, Map (4)
1902, pp. 6, Map (3)
1903, pp. 23, Maps (3) and (5)
1904, pp. 32, 7 plates, maps (3a) and (3b)
1905, pp. 19, Map (6)
1906, pp. 20, Map (6a)
1907, pp. 14, Map (6a)
1908, pp. 30, Map (6a)
1909, pp. 23, Map (6b)
1910, pp. 28, Map (7)
1911, pp. 20, Map (7)
1912, pp. 20, Map (8)
1913, pp. 40, Map (8)
1914, pp. 36, Map (8)
1915, pp, 36, Map (8)

Maps of the Yosemite National Park accompanying the reports are as follows:

1) By Lt. N. F. McClure, February 1895. 1 in. = 4 mi. 39 × 46 cm.
2) By Lt. H. C. Benson, 1897. 1 in. = 4 mi. 27 × 35 cm.
3) By Lt. N. F. McClure. March 1896. 3 in. = 8 mi. 41 × 20½ cm.
3a) Same as (3) marked to show game and cattle ranges.
3b) Same as (3) marked to show posts and routes of patrols.
4) By Lt. J. J. McMullen. 1901. 26 × 34 cm.
5) Map showing patented lands. 1903. 1 in. = 1½ mi. 66 × 89 cm.
6) By Frank Bond. 1905. 1 in. = 2 mi. 62 × 68 cm.
6a) Same as (6) except slight changes in boundary markings, and legend "Approved June 11, 1906."

6b) Similar to (6) but lacks hachures.
7) By U. S. Geological Survey. April 1910. 1/125,000, contours 100 ft. 69 × 72½ cm.
8) Travel-guide map. 1 in. = 6 mi. 22½ × 19 cm.

Unlike the Yellowstone Act, of March 1, 1872, by which Congress reserved and withdrew certain lands and set them apart "as a public park or pleasuring ground for the benefit and enjoyment of the people," the Yosemite Act, of October 1, 1890, merely reserved and withdrew certain lands in the region surrounding the Yosemite Valley and set them apart "as reserved forest lands." Nothing was said about "a public park," nor was the name "Yosemite National Park" used in the Act. The reservation was placed under the exclusive control of the Secretary of the Interior, who was empowered to make rules and regulations for its care and management. The regulations were to "provide for the preservation from injury of all timber, mineral deposits, natural curiosities or wonders within said reservation, and their retention in their natural condition." Subsequent acts of Congress, including appropriations, as well as the regulations and the reports of the acting superintendents, used the name "Yosemite National Park" and it was thus known by common consent and custom until, in an Act of February 7, 1905, excluding certain lands, the words, "which shall hereafter be known as the 'Yosemite National Park,' " are used. It was not until the Act of August 25, 1916, by which the National Park Service was established, that a legislative definition of purposes applicable to Yosemite, as to all other national parks, appears in the words: "To conserve the scenery and the natural and historic objects and the wild life therein and to provide for the enjoyment of the same in such manner and by such means as will leave them unimpaired for the enjoyment of future generations."

No appropriation for management and protection of the reservation was made by the Act of October 1, 1890, or by any legislation immediately following. Without funds and without personnel, the Secretary of the Interior called upon the War Department for assistance, and in May, 1891, Troop I, Fourth Cavalry, U. S. Army, Captain A. E. Wood in command, was designated guard for the Yosemite National Park. Thereafter, until the transfer to civilian administration in June, 1914, except for the Spanish War year of 1898, a cavalry officer was annually designated as "Acting Superintendent." In 1898 the post was taken, in turn, by an Inspector of the Interior Department and a Captain of Utah Volunteer Cavalry.

The problems confronting these cavalry officers were quite different from those that now pertain to the park. Foremost was the prevention of "trespass," which usually meant the unauthorized grazing of sheep and cattle. Captain Wood, in his initial report, states that at the opening of the summer of 1891 there were 60,000 sheep close to the southern border and 30,000 more near the western boundaries of the park about to enter. The situation was complicated by lack of maps and of information about the topography, the presence of large areas of patented land within the boundaries, and the knowledge—which soon got about—that there were no legal penalties for violations. The Act did provide that all persons trespassing upon the reservation could be removed therefrom, and the resourceful Army officers made good use of this provision by the simple plan of taking sheepherders into custody at one extremity of the park and ejecting them at the other. The loss of sheep for a week or more increasingly served as a deterrent.

Hunting was also a trespass, and firearms were forbidden within the boundaries without special permission. Violations of the regulations were frequent, however, during the first decade. One such violation was very badly timed, for it occurred under the superintendency of a very capable and caustic colonel, Samuel B. M. Young, who had fought through the Civil War and many Indian campaigns. Certain residents of San Francisco applied for a permit to carry arms into the park "for protection." The permit was refused, but an escort of soldiers was offered. The ensuing events are set forth in a little 16-page pamphlet entitled, "In the Department of the Interior. In the matter of the complaint of John L. Howard, et al., against Col. S. B. M. Young, U. S. A. Superintendant of the Yosemite National Park, California." (I saw two copies of this pamphlet in 1923, but they seem to have disappeared. A transcript, however, is in my notes.) The body of the text is a letter apparently addressed to the Secretary of War by Colonel Young, dated November 30, 1896. It relates the circumstances of finding the complainants within the park in possession of rifles and pistols. They were "duly removed." They complained to the highest authorities. Two passages quoted from Colonel Young's reply are gems that should not be allowed to vanish from sight.

"As to the personnel of the complainants, as set forth in the complaint, admitting specifically that they are severally members of various social and luncheon clubs as stated . . . , and admitting further that their social, commercial and financial standing is as high as their respective descriptive lists seem to intimate, I am unable to see that the facts so stated and admitted are in any way or in any degree relevant to the subject matter of their complaint. If they are relevant, I might plead in reply a list of clubs and other organizations with which I have had the honor to be associated. This I see no reason to do. If they believed that by reason of their exalted social, commercial and professional standing the rules of the Park would not be enforced against them, the experience of the complainants should have undeceived them."

And, in conclusion: "The letter of Mr. George C. Perkins, U. S. Senator from California, which accompanies this complaint and is referred to me therewith, is worthy of the serious attention of the Department. There is no reason why Mr. Perkins should not vouch for the social standing and credit of these complainants in support of their own averments on that point. But when Mr. Perkins, on a statement of facts made by one side only, goes so far out of his way as to denounce my conduct as 'hasty, ill-considered, and very reprehensible,' he is guilty of gross injustice. . . . If I had any doubt as to the character of the complaint and of those by whom it is preferred, it would be removed by this open and scandalous attempt to influence the judicial action of the Secretary by the official influence of a Senator in Congress."

A park superintendent challenging a United States Senator thus! What dire fate befell him? Within two years he was a major general commanding a division in the Spanish-American War and not hesitant about calling down a lieutenant colonel of Rough Riders for his men's boisterous conduct. In 1903 he became a lieutenant general, and President Roosevelt made him Chief of Staff!

Colonel Young's report on his superintendency was written before this episode took place. He had a good deal to say, however, as did his successors, about trespassing, fires, and, constructively, the planting of fish. The mapping of the park occupied the attention of the Army patrols, and a succession of maps was produced by the junior officers. Those of Lieutenant H. C. Benson and Lieutenant N. F. McClure, published in the reports, were the best maps of the region and were widely used until superseded in 1910 by those of the U. S. Geological Survey.

Enlargement and reduction of the park area, roads, and, especially, private lands were other subjects that occupied the attention of the superintendents. The boundaries were changed by Act of February 7, 1905, and again by Act of June 11, 1906, as is shown on the map accompanying the report for 1906. Privately owned lands within the park were greatly reduced by these boundary changes, but many remained to vex the administration, and all have not yet been acquired for the benefit of the public. The rights of private owners were asserted very vigorously by John B. Curtin, who owned land at Gin Flat and Crane Flat and other places. He brought suit against Colonel Harry C. Benson, Acting Superintendent from 1906 to 1908. The Circuit Court for the Northern District of California upheld Benson, but this decree was reversed in 1911 by the United States Supreme Court (*Curtin* v. *Benson,* 222 U. S. 78).

Biographical memoirs of Benson and McClure, who figure largely in these reports, will be found in the *Sierra Club Bulletin* (1925, Vol. 12, No. 2, pp. 175–179, and 1943, Vol. 28, No. 3, pp. 96–98, respectively). In *One Hundred Years in Yosemite,* by Carl Parcher Russell (Stanford University Press, 1931; revised edition, University of California Press, 1947), there is a chapter on "Administration under State and Federal Regulation"—in the new edition the title is "Guardians of the Scene." In *Yosemite Nature Notes* (June, 1944, Vol. 23, No. 6) there is an article, "Administrative Officers of Yosemite," by C. Frank Brockman, Park Naturalist.

25 *Reports of the Superintendents of Sequoia National Park*

Report of the Acting Superintendent of the Sequoia and General Grant National Parks to the Secretary of the Interior. [Year]

Washington: Government Printing Office. [Year]

(Variations in Title: for 1891, "Sequoia National Park," only; for 1895 to 1905, "California," or "in California," or "in the State of California," follows "National Parks"; for 1913, "Report on the Sequoia and General Grant National Parks"; for 1914 and 1915, "Superintendent.")

Included in annual reports of the Secretary of the Interior; also issued separately with printed paper wrappers. Approximately 23 × 15 cm.

Twenty-four numbers, as follows:

1891, pp. 10, Map (1)
1892, pp. 25
1893, pp. 17, Map (2)
1894, pp. 20
1895, pp. 8
1896, pp. 6
1897, pp. 7, Map (3)
1898, no report issued
1899, pp. 12, Map (4)
1900, pp. 11, 17 plates, Map (3a)
1901, pp. 10, 14 plates
1902, pp. 17, 15 plates, Map (5)
1903, pp. 18, Maps (3a), (6), (7)
1904, pp. 15, Maps (5a), (3a)
1905, pp. 19, Map (4a)
1906, pp. 11, Map (3b)
1907, pp. 11, Map (3b)
1908, pp. 19, 3 plates, Map (3b)
1909, pp. 17, Map (8)
1910, pp. 21, Map (8)
1911, pp. 21, Map (8a)
1912, pp. 16
1913, pp.16, Map (9)
1914, pp. 22, Map (9)
1915, pp. 24, Map (9)

Maps accompanying the reports are as follows:

1) Seven Townships. 1 in. = 6 mi. 21 × 18 cm.
2) Proposed Extension. 35 × 20 cm.
3) By Lt. M. F. Davis. 1896. 38 × 35 cm.
3a) Similar to (3), but reëngraved, with slight changes.
3b) Similar to (3a), but with additional data.
4) By Lt. H. B. Clark. 1899. 40 × 40 cm.
5) By I. N. Chapman. 1899–1900. 1 in. = 120 chains. 58 × 41 cm.

5b) Same as (5) with soldier camps in red.
6) Appropriated Lands. 2/3 in. = 1 mi. 48 × 40 cm.
7) Route of March. 1903. 1 in. = 16 mi. 17 × 43 cm.
8) U. S. Geological Survey. June, 1909. 1/125,000. Contours 100 ft. 64 × 41 cm.
8a) Same as (8) with additions. March, 1910. Same size.
9) Travel-guide Map. 1⅜ in. = 5 mi. 24 × 19 cm.

In the administration of Sequoia and General Grant national parks the cavalry officers who acted as superintendents encountered some of the same problems as those in Yosemite, but with differences owing to the character of the terrain and the predominance of the Big Trees. The park was established primarily to preserve these trees. After ten years of effort a bill was passed by Congress and signed by President Harrison, September 25, 1890. Less than a week later the park was more than doubled in size, and the General Grant Grove was added, by a section hastily attached to the Yosemite bill. Secretary of the Interior Noble shortly afterward gave the parks their names. An outline of events is given in "Legislative History of Sequoia and Kings Canyon National Parks," by Francis P. Farquhar (*Sierra Club Bulletin*, 1941, Vol. 26, No. 1, pp. 42–58).

In the very first annual report, Captain Joseph H. Dorst states the two themes that run through the series: "The Government, at whatever cost, should never allow any private individual or corporation to have control of any portion of this forest, nor allow any timber to be cut in it. As it stands now, and as it ought to remain, it is probably the most remarkable forest of its kind in the world. The more one sees of it the grander it seems. To despoil it would be a desecration." The other theme was the desirability of extending the park to include the mountainous country to the east in order to prevent denudation by sheep grazing and timber cutting from impairing the water supply. In 1892, Captain Dorst reports: "It is estimated that during the summer no less than 500,000 sheep have been feeding in the Kern and Kings River valleys." Captain Parker, in 1894, sums up the results: "As a consequence the country is entirely denuded of grass and bushes and presents a barren, uninviting aspect. But this is not all the damage the sheep have done. The soil, being denuded of grass, is broken up by thousands of sheep tracks, and when the rains come this loose soil is washed down the mountain sides into the valleys, covering up the swamps and meadows, destroying these natural reservoirs."

The way in which land was acquired within the area of the parks before the enactment of park and forest reserve legislation is a story yet to be written. Suffice it to say that as late as 1915 some of the finest trees and meadows in the Giant Forest, the very heart of Sequoia National Park, were in private ownership. Some of the patents had been granted in the decade of the 1880's, when the Kaweah Co-operative Commonwealth Colony hopefully proposed to sustain itself by lumber operations. With the collapse of that enterprise the patented lands remained in individual hands and continued as a threat against the park idea until the most important holdings were purchased and turned over to the Government through the efforts and generosity of the National Geographic Society and of Stephen T. Mather and a group of citizens inspired by him. ("History of the Kaweah Colony, 1885–1891," by George W. Stewart, in the *Weekly Visalia Delta,* November and December, 1891; "Kaweah. How and Why the Colony Died," by its President, Burnette G. Haskell, in *Out West,* September, 1902; "The Kaweah Experiment in Co-operation," by William Carey Jones, in the *Quarterly Journal of Economics,* October, 1891; *The Commonwealth: A Journal for Those Who Labor and Who Think,* Burnette G. Haskell, editor and publisher, San Francisco, 1889; *National Geographic Magazine,* January, 1917, pp. 1–11, and July, 1921, p. 85–86).

In the summer of 1896, Lieutenant Milton F. Davis (Brigadier General and Chief of Staff of the Army Air Service in World War I, and later head of the New York Military Academy) made a map of the entire region, from Kings Canyon to the Kern, which for a number of years thereafter formed a useful supplement to the reports of the superintendents. Lieutenant Henry B. Clark made a similar map in 1899.

The preservation of the mountainous regions east of the park, so urgently advocated by the first superintendents, was not accomplished in full for many years, although the grazing of sheep was gradually curtailed. The Kern River and Mount Whitney region was added to Sequoia National Park by Act of Congress approved July 3, 1926; and, by the Act of March 4, 1940, Kings Canyon National Park was established, absorbing the little General Grant National Park and making a continuous extensive area of Sequoia and Kings Canyon national parks.

There are probably very few complete collected sets of the Yosemite and Sequoia superintendents' reports in existence. Most of these annual reports are on file in the office of the Superintendent in the respective parks, and in many large libraries they may be found in the annual reports of the Secretary of the Interior.